Castles of Our Conscience

Castles of Our Conscience

Social Control and the American State, 1800–1985

William G. Staples

 Rutgers University Press
New Brunswick, New Jersey

First published in the United States of America by Rutgers University Press, 1991

First published in the United Kingdom by Polity Press in association with Basil Blackwell, 1990

Copyright © 1990 by William G. Staples

Library of Congress Cataloging-in-Publication Data

Staples, William G.
  Castles of our conscience: social control and the American
state, 1800–1985/William G. Staples.
      p.   cm.
  Includes bibliographical references and index.
  ISBN 0-8135-1626-9
  1. United States—Social policy.   2. Social control—History.
  3. Prison administration—United States—History.   4. Social
  service—United States—History.   I. Title.
  HN57.S68   1991
  361.6′ 1′ 0973—dc20   90-37620
                                                              CIP

Typeset in 11 on 13 pt Bembo by
Wearside Tradespools, Fulwell, Sunderland
Printed in Great Britain by Billing and Sons Ltd., Worcester

For Ian, joie de vivre

Contents

Preface

During the last 20 years or so two separate yet parallel discourses have matured and flourished in both sociology and history. One has been a renewed interest in "the state" as a theoretical and empirical focus of analysis. Here we have witnessed a reopening of the classical projects on the nature and consequences of the rise of modern nation states. The debates have been both forthright and stimulating, engendering some of the best comparative-historical social science in years. Meanwhile, students of law, crime, and deviance began a critical, "revisionist" intellectual movement which shifted the analysis of these social phenomena away from questions of individual conformity to issues of control. Indeed, the concept of "social control" became the organizing theme for a broader emphasis on power, politics, and economics. Yet while revisionist authors have moved the state into the forefront of their discussions, those analyses of social control that have appeared have tended to be "society-centered" rather than "state-centered" – the former being reductionistic, deriving the state from other structures within civil society – the latter assuming a degree of state autonomy with a logic and interest of its own. As I see it, there is a need to bring the full power and scope of a state-centered approach to bear on the historical theme of changing institutional social control practice. This is the intent of this book.

Certainly one great pleasure of completing this book is acknowledging those friends and colleagues that gave of their time and energy. Like most first books, this monograph began life as a dissertation and I want to thank the people at the University of Southern California who made that step possible. They include Jon Miller, Michael Dear, Daniel Glaser, Sol Kobrin, and, unfortunately posthumously, Robert Hodge. The process of converting some reasonable ideas into a book took place during my two-year appointment as a Post Doctoral Fellow at the University of California, Los Angeles. Here I was fortunate to share ideas and friendship with a number of people but especially Robert Emerson, Christine Grella, Oscar Grusky, Kathleen Montgomery, Michael Mann, Melvin Pollner, William Roy, Judith Stepan-Norris, and Maurice Zeitlin. I own a great debt, both in intellectual and in practical terms, to Michael Dear and Anthony Giddens. Not only has their work profoundly influenced my own thinking, but their advice, support, and confidence in the project was unfailing.

I am grateful as well to those institutions and organizations which help support my work. They include the Department of Sociology and the Social Science Research Institute of the University of Southern California, UCLA, the National Institute of Mental Health, and, finally, the Rockefeller Foundation for my time spent at the Bellagio Study Center in Lake Como, Italy in the spring of 1985.

Few people have shared more in my personal and intellectual life than my brother and fellow sociologist, Cliff Staples. I thank him dearly for his encouragement, and most of all his friendship, which deepens as the years go by. Contributing her keen sociological imagination and her ability to tirelessly read draft upon draft of my coarse prose, Carol Warren has given much of herself to this book. I thank her for all her help. This book is dedicated to my son Ian Warren Staples, for our Tuesdays together, for teaching me not to take myself too seriously, and for showing me what is really important in this world. You are, indeed, the joy of my life.

W. G. Staples
Lawrence, Kansas

Introduction

It is for the other world that the madman sets sail in his fool's boat; it is from the other world that he comes when he disembarks. The madman's voyage is at once a rigorous division and an absolute Passage . . . He is put in the interior of the exterior, and inversely. A highly symbolic position, which will doubtless remain his until our own day, if we are willing to admit that what was formerly a visible fortress of order has now become the castle of our conscience.

Michel Foucault★
Madness and Civilization

★ Reproduced by kind permission of Vintage Books, a division of Random House Publishers.

1

Explaining Patterns of Institutional Social Control

From Progressivism to Revisionism

The history of public policy in the United States concerning the care and control of the ill, the dependent, the misbehaved and dangerous, has been a cyclical one of "reforms," "innovations," and "solutions." Until recently, a reformist historiography had assessed these policy movements as the result of shifts in ideological currents, often stressing the actions of benevolent, forward thinking progressives in shaping a more humane social world.[1] This was a history of progress, a history of unquestionable allegiance to scientific humanism and social intervention. Even if failure occurs, according to this vision, it is eventually overcome through the application of more resources, better training, planning and the like. Today, a body of revisionist history and sociology challenges this perspective with a "determination to locate the reform enterprise in the social, economic and political contexts of the period."[2]

Despite this common goal, however, revisionist accounts of the history of social control policies remain fractured along several fronts. These divisions involve basic debates concerning idealism vs. materialism, action vs. structure, and the historical place of human agency. Those who emphasize materialist interpretations of history focus on class, politics, and economics as determinants of social reforms and attempt to link these movements and the origins of institutions to structural changes such as urbanization, industrialization, and the rise of capitalism. Materialist views have, more often than not, placed agency in the hands of dominant classes and have characterized reformist policies as ultimately reflecting the "social control" interests of such classes.[3] Other materialist interpretations range from a focus on the fiscal constraints of the welfare state, to a concern with the historical ascendancy of discipline, surveillance, and classification in what Michel Foucault has characterized as an economy of "power."[4] Still others, such as David Rothman, writing from a more pluralist view, see the "discovery of the asylum" as a response to general disorder and disequilibrium in society rather than a threat to any particular social class.[5]

While revisionist writers have taken us beyond the "history of progress" paradigm, I argue that they have yet to offer a theoretically-guided analysis of the role of the state in the historical transformation of institutional social control. Here I am referring narrowly to those practices – from imprisonment to mental hospitalization – which remove people from the everyday life of society.[6] Paradoxically, this situation exists despite the fact that many contemporary revisionists take the centrality of the state as a given. As one group of authors recently put it, "It is obvious that a theory of the state must be central to any analysis of social control in . . . capitalist societies since the state has assumed direct responsibility for supporting the institutions of control."[7] And yet, many writers, in their attempt to unearth the "real" basis of social policies, have lost sight of the day-to-day realities of the state and the interests of those who administer these "institutions of control."

In actuality, revisionist writers have offered "society-centered" rather than "state-centered" inquiries. That is, within society-centered analyses – whether pluralist, Marxist, or otherwise – society is the initial and principal object of inquiry and the state is derived from or reduced to an arena of competing interest-group politics, a reflection of class relations, and the like.[8] Alternatively, more "structural" perspectives on the state have portrayed its existence and function as taking place "behind the backs" of actors. That is, action, and hence human

agency, is reduced to structural "adjustments" and the "imperatives" of capitalist production. A decade of debate among
theorists concerning the "relative autonomy" of the state has
yielded only minor concession to the idea of treating the state as
a *potentially* autonomous institution.[9]

Toward a State-centered Perspective

While not denying the insights of society-centered theories, I
wish to develop a view which acknowledges the appearance of,
and the necessity for, a distinct political sphere in society with a
separate logic and interest of its own. Such state "autonomy"
differentiates the state from civil society if only by the fact that
the state has the power to do things that other social groups can
not. Yet I also argue that in capitalist societies, the state has an
inter-dependent relationship with the economic and social/
cultural spheres. I therefore conceive of the state as having
unique, institutionalized power and authority which is, in turn,
embedded within the wider social formation. The purpose of
this state-centered approach is to focus on the actual performance of the state as an institution operating within a specific
socio-historical context.

Further, I wish to analyze the necessity of state intervention
within the context of contradiction and crisis management, and
assert an interpretive framework which explicitly assumes that
state managers have, with few exceptions, an institutionalized
self-interest in the reproduction of *both* the state and the wider
capitalist social formation; a dual investment which must be
constantly negotiated under changing historical contexts. State
managers and elites, in my view, are historical subjects whose
actions are not incidental to the history of public policy. I
therefore wish to account for the appearance, evolution, and
dissolution of various social control practices within the social
structuration of the state. Structure, in this view, is both the
medium and outcome of social practice – the action of capable
and knowledgeable human agents.[10] Therefore, if the purpose

of this book is to understand changing US institutional control practice in terms of the origins and activities of the state, it is necessary to delineate the multiple dimensions of "the state." What is the state? What does it do? How does it operate? How is it reproduced across time and social space? And what is the basis of its power? Answers to these questions form the basis of my state-centered approach.

The Structuration of the State: Form, Function, and Apparatus

In the most general of terms, a common and useful conception of the modern state is contained in Weber's four key elements: a differentiated set of institutions and personnel embodying; centrality in the sense that political relations radiate outward from a center to cover; a territorially demarcated area, over which it exercises; a monopoly of authoritative binding rule-making, backed up by a monopoly of the means of physical violence. Hence the state may be characterized as an administrative, legal, bureaucratic, and coercive organization possessing a unique form of power. Michael Mann has argued that two types of power characterize modern states: "despotic" and "infrastructural" power. Despotic power is unlimited, autonomous state capacity undertaken without consultation with civil society while infrastructural power is the ability of the state to penetrate civil society and implement political decisions.[11] This study is principally an exploration of the infrastructural power of the American state.

Beyond this general definition, one could argue that there are three crucial dimensions to understanding any modern state and its activities: the historically specific *form* the state takes, the *functions* or activities it engages in, and the mechanisms or *apparatus* through which functions are executed. This form-function-apparatus logic sets out the theoretical agenda for a state-centered analysis and provides a conceptual bridge linking abstract state theory with a historical account of state organizations.[12] "Form" refers to how and why a specific state is constituted by, and evolves within, a given social formation. For example, most generally, we might distinguish several historically-based social formations: primitive, traditional, liberal-capitalist, and advanced-capitalist.[13] In traditional formations, the principle of organization is political/class domination, wrested from the previous kinship system; the central functions of power and control are vested in the state. In the liberal-capitalist formation, the basic structuring principles revolve around the relationship between wage labor and capital, anchored in civil law, which takes place in the "private" sphere of civil society. The liberal-capitalist state is primarily a decentralized and localized body. It is dependent on both the presence and continuity of private accumulation through its reliance on materials created in that process, on budgetary resources derived through taxation, and from the political legitimation it derives from maintaining this universe of commodity production.

Yet while dependent on private production, the liberal-capitalist state is excluded from directly organizing or coordinating commodity production. These conditions form the basic links between the economic sphere and the state. Such a "capitalist state" is not, however, reducible to capital itself. Increasingly, the process of private accumulation is equally dependent on the state as a coordinating, autonomous "corporate actor." This and other changes in the nature of class relations, the mode of production and the like signal the transformation to an advanced-capitalist formation and the rise of a new capitalist-state form. Thus, historically, we expect to observe a dynamic process between the state and the social formation whereby each transforms, and is transformed by, the other.

"Function" refers to those activities undertaken by and in the name of the state – that is, its operational objectives. In the most general sense, both liberal and advanced capitalist state managers have the mandate to recreate capitalist social relations. This includes taking steps to secure four basic conditions: *social consensus, economic production* and *social consumption*; and *social integration.* Social consensus is achieved by ensuring acceptance of the prevailing contract by all social groups. Only with such an accord can order, stability, and security exist. Here the state defines rules and laws governing ownership, property rights, provides for political representation, legal definitions of legitimate and illegitimate behavior, a judicial system of dispute resolution, and the like. By securing conditions of production, the state provides a framework within which the material basis of both capitalist social relations and the state itself may be reproduced. These provisions include a basic economic infrastructure (e.g. coinage, weights and measures, a transportation system, etc.), venture incentives, direct subsidies, and the legal framework of business activity, all of which reproduce investment capital and the legitimating support of those who control it.

Historically, the capitalist state has also been implicated in social consumption. The viability of commodity production is dependent on both the reproduction of labor power and the consumption of goods and services. The enactment of laws regulating despotism in the work place, length of the working day, and the establishment of a minimum wage all demonstrate the state's role as a coordinating and regulating body ensuring consumption. Finally, the capitalist state must affirm a degree of social integration by affording a minimum level of welfare for all groups. This is done through the redistribution of social wealth via tax laws, public education, and other "social services" and benefits. All four functions involve, in one way or another, the necessity of autonomous state action in the reproduction of both the state itself – in terms of political legitimacy and material power – as well as the wider social formation – in terms of coordinating economic exchange and ensuring the stability of class relations. Only in the most general sense am I arguing that the long-run viability of *any* capitalist state is dependent on its ability to obtain these goals. Clearly, and as the present analysis will demonstrate, the actual development of the state suggests a constant shifting of objectives and priorities in response to contingent crises and the competing claims by groups in and out of the state.

Execution of these goals by the state however is dependent on the existence of an adequate bureaucratic machinery. While the concept of the "state apparatus" has appeared in the literature for some time, there has been little attempt to clarify its theoretical and practical boundaries. In an effort to address this problem, Gordon Clark and Michael Dear have offered the following scheme: "state apparatus" refers to the mechanisms through which state power is exercised and state functions realized; "sub-apparatus" is the more specific term for the set of agencies, organizations, and institutions representing the actual mechanisms of state power and function; and "para-apparatus" references those subsidiary agencies which are technically outside the sphere of direct state control, but have financial, legal or organizational ties to the state apparatus.[14] These concepts imply a continuum of state power and organization – ranging from a "pure" form of sub-apparatus such as criminal courts – to a "para-apparatus" such as contemporary defense contractors.

Rather than a mere catalog of government agencies, the concept of the state apparatus is a key component of any state-centered analysis. The apparatus of the state represents the concrete form of state power. As such, it constitutes a bureaucratic medium which necessarily shapes and transforms the actual exercise of state power and capacity. Once established, such bureaucratic organizations may take on a logic and interest of their own, creating a "slippage" between their intended function and existence. This form of enfranchisement may create obsolescent organizations within the state and may distort the linkage between policy and implementation. Moreover, as a concrete form, the policies and activities of the apparatus are vulnerable to being influenced by outside groups with their own agenda. Not that such groups are capable of simply controlling a sub-apparatus of the state, but rather that it is possible to observe "sequences of alliances," more or less temporary and policy specific, between groups in and out of the state. Thus, not only must we explore the relationship between the state apparatus and state functions but we must comprehend their own internal organizational logic and inertia and the extent to which these organizations mediate the exercise of state power.

Table 1.1 outlines the approximate relationship between capitalist-state functions and their specific sub-apparatus.

Table 1.1   The capitalist-state apparatus

	Functions			
	Consensus	*Production*	*Integration*	*Executive*
Sub-apparatus	Political	Public production	Health, education and welfare	Administration
	Legal	Public provision	Information	Regulatory agencies
	Repressive	Treasury	Communications and media	

Adapted from Clark and Dear, *State Apparatus*, p. 50.

In addition to the four functions outlined above, the "executive" activity of the state appears in table 1.1 Rather than an operational objective per se, the executive sub-apparatus plays a role in coordinating and monitoring the reproduction of the state apparatus itself. Here is the primary location of administrative and regulatory activities based on managerial and technical expertise. In terms of the present study, a history of US institutional social control policies is an account of the evolution of the legal, repressive, and health and welfare sub-apparatus of the American state. In summary, I would argue that if we can come to discern the relationship between the form-function-apparatus dimensions of a particular state, we can begin to comprehend its historical trajectory and the policies and practices it engages in.

Because state personnel and officials play a significant role in initiating and reproducing state power via the state apparatus, I take them seriously as social agents and historical actors. Institutions of the state, like other social formations, are reproduced on a daily basis by the people who organize and run them. Rather than "bracket" their interests and motivations, a strategy common to many forms of "structural" analyses, I see their investment in the state as a powerful force shaping policies and outcomes. Thus I consider individuals who derive their principal occupational, professional, and material existence from the state as a social class not unlike any other. This class exhibits an internal hierarchy of power and interest – from elected politicians to career bureaucrats, to administrative, technical, and staff personnel. No matter what their position, state actors are social agents who draw upon the rules, power, authority, and material resources available to them in order to act in ways which reproduce the state and their place within it. This is not to say that state managers are so self-interested that they cannot be co-opted by interest groups vying to shape the state policy agenda. In this sense, the state is indeed an arena of class conflict. However, I would argue that it is unlikely that state officials would knowingly act in such a way which would threaten their positions in the state apparatus. Moreover, I do not assume that such officials possess superior knowledge and insight nor that their actions, while "rational," are necessarily successful.

Finally, like other social classes, state managers and personnel are rarely united on specific issues or policies. Their interests in the state are often fragmented relative to their location in the bureaucratic hierarchy and in terms of inter- and intra-agency competition for resources, organizational jurisdiction, and pro-fessional status. Political parties moreover, may provide the bases for fragmentation within the state class. This may occur through the confrontation of different parties over control of the state, or it may arise over the conflicting interests of an elected political regime and that of managers of the various sub-apparatus.

Given the functions of the state outlined above, and hence the necessity for state intervention, a central question remains: under what conditions are intercessions likely to occur? Historically, it would appear that it is during acute political, economic or social crises that the state is likely to intervene.[15] That is, it is during times of war, economic duress, or social upheaval that infrastructural state power may be most dramatically displayed. The state then plays a primary role in what Claus Offe calls the "crisis management" of capitalist societies and this role is dependent on the state's ability to penetrate civil society.[16] And yet the state intervenes on a more mundane or "routine" basis (often the lingering on of policies long after the precipitating "crisis" has ended), and this too reflects infrastructural power.[17] These interventions and the exercise of such power permits state managers to play a role in reproducing the economic and normative/cultural spheres of society. It is also the very basis of the social structuration of the state itself. That is, the encroachment of the state into everyday life reflects not just crisis management, but state reproduction. As I have pointed out above, agencies of the state apparatus become entrenched, taking on a life and interest of their own, thus creating a tension between securing the objectives of the state and ensuring the survival of the apparatus.

Techniques for survival vary. A state sub-apparatus may expand its organizational or jurisdictional domain by absorbing other state functions or organizations or it may capture what were once "civil" regulatory functions. On the other hand, the state may subordinate previously independent or "private" organizations or institutions, and thereby extend its control and authority. This so called "statization" process reflects not simply an aggregation or expansion of the state apparatus, by rather implies a significant reconstitution of political power and presupposes a dynamic and fluid relationship between the state and civil society.

What are the limits of state intervention? Clearly there are fiscal, administrative, legal, and organizational constraints on "successful" state action. Yet there are also limits in the form of contradictions embedded in interventionist strategies themselves – that is, in the form, function and apparatus of the state.

Therefore, it is within the policy-making *capacity* of the American state that I focus my analysis of the changing practices of institutional social control. While the capitalist state form is enmeshed in the economic contradictions of private accumulation, it is also challenged by its own cumulative self-obstruction. This predicament arises from the fact that the state is increasingly drawn into both economic and social life in an attempt to mediate crises and impart rationality. Yet such interventions may ultimately violate the other principles of state reproduction and threaten to exacerbate present problems or generate new ones. A contradiction in this sense is an opposing or disjunctive condition to the structuring principles necessary for social reproduction. That is, both the form of a given state and the operational objectives of consensus, production, and integration are not necessarily congruous, but rather are potentially contradictory. For example, the provision of a redistributive tax system to secure integration might reduce investments and therefore curtail private production.

The state apparatus exhibits internal, contradictory tendencies as well. As I have argued, organizations become moribund, perpetuating themselves rather than adapting to new policy directions. Thus obsolete agencies may co-exist alongside new ones, distorting intervention strategies and policy goals. There is a tension between the demand for centralized control and that of decentralized flexibility. And, finally, an ever-expanding state apparatus may begin to consume increasing amounts of state resources thereby creating potential fiscal crises.

The logic of my theory/method is that contradictions of state action, embedded in each period, engender new problems requiring further action but under new historical circumstances. Thus subsequent policy initiatives reflect adjustments to the accumulated contradictions of past actions and the attempt by state managers to balance their objectives with the material, legal, and administrative capacities available to them. Thus two fundamental themes guide my analysis: (1) that state policies reflect the actions of knowledgeable, capable human agents involved in social reproduction and (2) that such meaningful actions are always bounded by unacknowledged conditions and the unintended consequences of previous action.

My theoretical agenda implies a multilevel analysis. First, at the compositional level, I endeavor to account for the interaction between changes in the economic and social/cultural spheres and the constitution and functions of the state. These are the structural properties of the social system embedded in the *longue duree* of social reproduction that both enable and constrain human action. At the more concrete, contextual level, I examine the strategic conduct of social actors – in and out of the state – in the day-to-day reproduction of the *duree* of the state apparatus. I explore the history of institutional social control in the United States, synthesizing primary and secondary material into a historical narrative. The two parts (chapters 2–6) cover roughly the periods 1800–1929 and 1930–1985. These periods highlight major developments in the form, function, and apparatus of the American state which are reflected in the changing modes and strategies of social control policies.

In seeking to provide a theoretically-informed analysis of these very complex developments, I have set myself a challenging agenda. Clearly the ambitiousness of this project calls for a few caveats. Whenever someone attempts to survey such a broad sweep of history, eyebrows are raised, and indeed, they should be. I have undoubtedly left myself open to charges of "historically-insensitivity," of misplacing facts, and of distorting chronology. Yet, while such accusations may turn out to be correct, I hope they will be excused as minor infractions when judged against what is gained by looking at the long-term processes of social change. Moreover, history tends to be a rather recalcitrant partner in our attempt to parcel it into neat periods or to use theoretical concepts to frame or label it. I have no illusion that the periodization I offer, or that the constructs I employ, provide a perfect correspondence with recorded events.

Finally, since my primary goal is to provide a meaningful interpretation of broad historical patterns, I am less concerned with the task of doing primary historical research than I am with linking both new and existing data. This is not an excuse for conducting shoddy historiography – inaccurate or otherwise – but rather reflects the differing task of the sociologist pursuing historically informed analyses, and the historian elucidating original data from primary sources. Therefore since the history I am studying is, in parts, relatively well studied and documented, I have relied on both primary and secondary materials in developing my narrative. My use of these secondary sources is intended to establish historical "facts" and events and in no way implies an adoption or intended synthesis of these authors' diverse theoretical views or assumptions.

PART I

The Denial of Freedom in the New Republic

Social Control and the American State, 1800–1929

2

Charting the Liberal-Capitalist State

In chapter one it was argued that in order to understand the historical evolution of the state apparatus it is appropriate to first address the question of form – how and why a specific state is constituted by, and evolves within, a given social and historical context – and second, that we consider those activities undertaken by and in the name of the state – that is, its functions. The purpose of this section is to characterize the changing form and function of the American liberal-capitalist state from roughly 1800 to the 1930s. Two basic state forms are revealed during this period. The first was the "Accumulative State," a transition state reflecting a compromise between the new liberalism and the old order which took an active role in ensuring economic development and establishing public order until about 1860.[1] The second was the "Bureaucratic State" which resulted, on the one hand, from the very success of the Accumulative State, and on the other hand, from a fundamental "realignment" between political parties and state apparatus. Once a clear picture of state form and function is developed, a historical analysis of the state social control apparatus is possible.

The Accumulative State

The Articles of Confederation, adopted by the original thirteen colonies in 1781, failed to provide an adequate legal framework for successful economic development and thus threatened to undermine the establishment of legitimate authority in the revolutionary republic. Dissatisfaction with the Articles erupted during the depression of the 1780s when it became clear to those known as the "Federalists" that a more powerful national government was necessary for effective development; indeed to provide for "a more perfect Union." Thus the Constitution emerged as a framework to address the shortcomings of the Articles. The objectives of the Federalists included the creation of a single, coin currency, a goal which would remove the power of the states to print paper money, to forgive debtors, and to inhibit commercial contracts there by creating a more uniform commercial environment. They sought to create a political body with the power to enlarge foreign markets, stimulate domestic manufacture, issue public securities, to exploit natural resources, and to protect the rights of property owners from slave revolts and other social insurrections. Most importantly, and much of the rest of the agenda depended on it, Congress was granted independent taxing power.[2]

Therefore, like many "new" states, a claim to legitimate political authority depended on demonstrated effectiveness, particularly in terms of economic performance and the preservation of public order. Creating and defining the parameters to transform "merchantalist custom into capitalist practice" was a primary function of the early (1790–1860) American state form.[3] With the aid of the Constitution, the emerging national government provided the broadest possible canvas for economic development; it was up to state governments to complete the portrait. State intervention for the sake of economic development took a number of direct and dramatic forms during the period, while other strategies were more subtle.

The most dramatic examples were in creating the country's transportation, banking, and some of its large commercial enterprises such as paper mills and glass houses. Mechanism for development included lotteries, relaxed tax laws, direct subsidies, the granting of franchises which sheltered new companies from competition, chartering banks and corporations, partnership and even direct state ownership of banks, railroads, and even businesses.[4] More subtle, but none the less critically important techniques included the inspection of products, standardization of trading practices, safeguarding and regulating natural resources and the like. The principle of *laissez-faire*, so closely identified with the nineteenth century, became a dominant ideology only *after* the sufficient growth of private sources of capital. The Accumulative State, then, was an interventionist state. It extended itself into diverse social and economic arrangements creating the basis for both capitalist development and the conditions of its own reproduction.

A second goal of the Accumulative State was the establishment of social consensus *vis-a-vis* order, stability, and security. Two important features characterize Colonial and early American practices of dealing with deviance and criminality: public ritual and the social exclusion. Public ceremonies involving torture, branding, and mutilation served to define community standards of behavior; moreover, the deviant was effectively labelled, reputationally if not physically, as an outcast to townspeople and strangers alike. Likewise, while local dependents – paupers, orphans, the mentally and physically ill and the like – were, in lieu of family support, deserving of town alms in post-revolutionary America, outsiders attempting to obtain sustenance were summarily expelled. By the turn of the nineteenth century, however, the public spectacle of deviance control began to fade and an alternative form of exclusion took hold. At that time, the state began to exercise its legal powers to deprive citizens of their freedom by placing them in public institutions. What brought about this change in policy? A few factors seem critical in fostering the trend towards institutionalization.[5]

The first was the necessity that the new republic separate itself from the vestiges of British rule and establish its own legitimate authority. Many at that time argued that new democratic institutions were needed to reflect the spirit of republican rule. Indeed, as Benjamin Rush, a leading intellectual of the day, contended, the citizens of a constitutional system needed to be morally fabricated, by new (the asylum and the penitentiary) and existing (family, school and church) institu-

tions, into "republican machines" who would, as Thomas
Dumm phrased it, "fit the demands required by such a form of
government."[6] A prime target of criticism was the inherited
English Common Law and, in particular, its criminal statutes
which were a constant reminder of monarchical oppression.
But changes were not immediate. It took more than 30 years for
states to enact modifications in criminal codes which reduced
physical punishment. Yet beyond the revolutionary rhetoric
and the humanitarian crusade to abolish physical punishment,
was the fact the continued use of Common-law statutes involving "cruel" sanctions were not applied consistently thus making
criminal justice arbitrary and ineffectual. "A jury, squeezed
between two distasteful choices, death or acquittal, often
acquitted the guilty" according to Lawrence Friedman.[7] Both
the lingering association with English Common Law and this
kind of "jury lawlessness" (often provoking vigilante justice)
endangered the establishment of rational-legal authority, and
threatened to create more disorder than order.

Moreover, increases in immigration, urbanization, and commerce occurring between the Revolution and the 1830s had
specific consequences in undermining the use of ceremonial
social control and non-institutional methods and, in turn,
fostering the search for alternatives. These trends tended to
break down the distinctions between townsfolk and strangers
and thus the social cohesiveness of communities. This was
clearly evident in bustling seaport towns and cities displaying
increasing gaps between rich and poor, but was also present in
the surrounding countryside as outlying villages were drawn
into the cities' social and economic web. Urbanization, shifting
populations, and immigration diminished the effectiveness of
stigmatizing by public shaming rituals, while, at the same time,
these ceremonies themselves became a potential source of civil
disobedience and disorder. In Philadelphia, for example, the
application of the city's "wheelbarrow" law of 1786 put
shaven-headed, ragged, chain-gang prisoners to work cleaning
the streets under the watchful eye of armed guards. Not only
was the sight of these men distasteful to the good citizens of the
city as the convicts went about "begging and insulting the

inhabitants, [and] collecting crowds of idle boys," but they became the sport of others who tormented the prisoners incessantly.[8] The law of March 27, 1789 soon sequestered prisoners to conditions of more "private" punishment at the Walnut Street jail.

In the case of dependency, townsfolk became less willing to take in and board strangers while at the same time, those that would, demanded more and more compensation. Coupled with increased numbers and costs, rural residents shifted from a system of direct citizen aid to the poorhouse. Robert Cray states, in a detailed study of poor relief in New York State, that "Old methods of assisting needy persons, with their emphasis on community participation, were frequently cast aside by local officials in a frenzied effort to find more economical means of sheltering them. In the process, rural poor people came to be viewed less as objects of charity and more as costly burdens."[9] The cities, having first experienced the effects of population expansion, had turned to the poorhouse as early as 1700. The historical evidence suggests, however, that the first four decades after the revolution were a period of transition where Colonial practices of law, custom, and social control existed alongside republican ones.

Between the 1820s and mid-century an accelerated adoption of institutional arrangements occurred with an unprecedented expansion of the various states' existing penal and welfare sub-apparatus, primarily in the form of the penitentiary and the poorhouse.[10] If the public ritual aspect of social control had become obsolete, the advantages of social isolation in institutions had become that much more powerful within the emerging political and economic order. The activities of the Accumulative State which took an active role in developing economic expansion created a nation characterized by Friedman as a "republic of bees." Here law was used to "further the interests of the middle-class *mass*, to foster growth, [and] to release and harness the energy latent in the commonwealth . . ."[11] The vast expansion of such a propertied class had specific consequences for state social control policy. Not only was the legitimacy of the state dependent on its ability to protect the property of such a burgeoning class, but their existence pressured state officials to respond to the desire of "respectable" people, according to Christopher Lasch, "to insulate themselves from the spectacle of suffering and depravity and avoid the contamination of the lower orders."[12] Moreover, the activities of the Accumulative State were intended, in part, to create a more uniform administrative sub-apparatus and an ordered private economic sphere by developing transportation links and encouraging the inter- and intra-state flow of goods, labor and capital. This had the consequence reducing the extent to which communities could insulate themselves by banishing the suspected deviant or needy through settlement laws, and made the almshouse an attractive option for the creation of social isolation.[13]

This emerging political and economic order demanded a single standard of citizenship, one characterized by self-reliance and support, industriousness, and thrift, which distinguished those at the core of social life from those on its margins. Articulated most powerfully in the rhetoric of reformers, the penitentiary and the poorhouse would isolate the marginalized (i.e. those not possessing such virtues or property) and transform them into ideal citizens or, in Rush's terms, into "republican machines." At the same time, reformers contended that the institutions would be fiscally and administratively more palatable than the older methods. Such a vision was eagerly embraced by public officials anxious to curtail rising costs and to respond to the perceived increases in crime and dependency.

In summary, what I want to argue is that beyond "Enlightenment" ideas and the rhetoric of reform, fundamental demographic, social, political, and economic changes were altering the formation of American life in the early mid-nineteenth century that were undermining older practices of social control and engendering new ones.[14] Pre-Revolutionary practices of law and social control served to reproduce colonial rule and the political structure of the *ancien régime*. In the post-Revolutionary period, however, these practices either withered away or were integrated into new forms of social control which were grounded within the historically-specific rise of the American liberal-capitalist state. The accumulative-oriented activities of this "new" interventionist state form had the affect of accelerating the breakdown of community cohesiveness and isolation and hence the practicality and effectiveness of non-institutional social control. Still charged with securing social consensus and a minimum level of integration – achieved in part, through its legal, judicial and public welfare practices – local and state governments erected an institutionally-based social control apparatus to perform these functions. The consequences and contradictions of this action forms the basis of the remainder of this and subsequent chapters.

The Bureaucratic State

The structure of the American economy and polity changed dramatically in the post-Civil War period. The factory system, rather than commercial agriculture, would become the cornerstone of an industrialized urban nation. From an economy characterized by small-scale enterprises controlled by families, individuals, and partners, rose the trust and the holding company, legal entities which served to eliminate market competition. Indeed, the period from about the 1860s to the 1920s saw the rise of monopoly capital. Yet rapid economic development was interspersed with bouts of depression, unemployment, and violent social unrest. The period was characterized by a dominant *laissez-faire* ideology, political corruption, and eventually, muckraking journalism and social reform. Building social consensus and securing social integration became primary functions of the state.

While monopolies dominated the market place, the seeds of centralization took hold in the state as well. Reformers attacked the corruption of the party patronage or "spoils" system, advocating revision of civil service procedures and accountabilities like the Pendleton Act and bipartisan representation on commissions and boards.[15] Such "rationalizing" reforms were intended to make the administrative apparatus of the state more efficient and manageable, and indeed, it became truly bureaucratic. Within the social control sub-apparatus, the process began with the founding of state boards of charities in the 1860s and was later fueled by the failure of public and private charities to respond to the crisis of the depression of 1893. With the election of 1896, an accelerated, Progressive restructuring of urban administration and public welfare bureaucracies took place. These organizations, and legions of new, urban professionals and "experts" running them, went about collecting information and statistics on crime, poverty and the like, and applied the rigors of science to the problem. One unintended consequence of this bureaucratic state building was an expansion of state power and organizational reach. As I will demonstrate in chapter 3, within the evolving social control sub-apparatus (principally the poorhouses, the insane asylums, and an array of "specialized" facilities), lower-tiered political entities such as local municipalities were increasingly overshadowed by the upper levels of the state hierarchy. This movement, I will argue, was the result of the state's role in crisis management, the need for a centralized agency to extend administrative rationality and planning and reflected a consolidation of political power. Thus centralization of state and public authority was as much about reproducing the state itself as it was about solving problems of deviancy and dependency. Before addressing these concerns, however, I want to first explore the evolution of the penal sub-apparatus and focus on *the* most important issue shaping the complexion of this state institution during the period: prison labor.

Production Politics in the Nineteenth-century Prison

The history of the state penitentiary during the nineteenth century provides an excellent illustration of the conflicts, problems, and contradictions encountered by an evolving sub-apparatus of the state. As I will demonstrate in this and other chapters, one strategy of state managers for confronting the fiscal, administrative, and organizational dilemmas of institutional social control has been the attempt to make inmates work for their keep. Nowhere is this strategy more evident than in the evolution of criminal justice sub-apparatus. Yet what little contemporary writing there has been on the development and use of penal labor in the nineteenth century has been dominated by society-centered revisionism which has failed to explain adequately the appearance, consequence, and ultimate dismantling of these production regimes.[16] Thus the theoretical questions at issue are: Why was it that, in the nineteenth century, the prison came to resemble the factory? Whose interest did this resemblance serve? And moreover, what accounts for the ultimate failure of the state to "industrialize" correctional facilities?

The "Problem" of Prison Labor

It cost Americans little to incarcerate criminals in the immediate post-Civil War period.[17] Most responsible was the use of inmate labor to defray costs. In fact, penal labor contributed to minimal outlays and balanced books and, in some cases, produced profits for most operations from roughly 1830 to the 1880s. However, by this later time, penologists, criminologists, legislatures, and the public were engaged in a debate about the conditions under which prisoners would work. For few doubted the notion that prisoners *should* work – that was a given. As one participant at the National Prison Association meetings of 1883 stated, "I take it for granted there are no gentlemen in this room that do not hold to the idea that there must be labor in prison. It is simply a matter of labor, or supporting the convicts in idleness."[18] And three years later, a Chicago Correctional Superintendent stated in his address to the National Prison Congress, "We are here today as scientists, reformers and business men. As such, in a trio sense, we are to discuss Prison Labor. We are agreed, that the physical employment by criminals is essential to their health, happiness, and

reform . . . But we are not agreed as to the system of employment . . . Economic questions largely control our views."[19]

Indeed, the "problem" of prison labor during the 1880s
centered on the question of under which system of production
the work would be organized. By 1885, roughly five "factory
regimes" existed for organizing production in America's prisons, reformatories, workhouses and jails.[20] According to the
Bureau of Labor Statistics these were: (1) the lease, (2) the
contract, (3) the piece-price, (4) the state-account and (5) the
state-use system.[21] While these regimes co-existed in some
states during the nineteenth century, the proportion of inmates
involved in each production system varied considerably over
time. A state-centered analysis suggests that the establishment
of the lease, contract, and piece-price arrangements reflected
various alliances created by state managers with private capital
in order to confront the problematic nature of institutional
policies for the liberal-capitalist state.

Under the lease system, inmate labor was sold to the highest
bidder for a fixed period. The state abdicated all responsibility
for prisoners to the lessee including food, shelter and control.
The system became widely adopted throughout the United
States, particularly in the south, as a substitute for African
slavery. The contract system was similarly embraced by prison
authorities. Under this regime, inmates toiled within the walls
of the prison in factory shops which were set up by the
administration, but were run by outside contractors and their
foremen. The contractor supplied the raw materials and paid
the state a fixed rate for every day worked and for the number
of prisoners employed. The piece-price, a variation on the
contract scheme, was adopted in only a few states. Here the
state retained complete control over the labor process. The
contractor provided the raw materials and manufacturing spe-
cifications but had no employees within the walls of the
institution. Inmate labor was sold by the number of pieces
produced.

Finally, two solely public arrangements were the state-
accounts and state-use systems. Under the state-accounts model
the state assumed, according to Louis Robinson, "the role of the

entrepreneur . . . entering fully into business with all its risk and uncertainties."[22] The state incurred capital costs, procured raw materials, organized and controlled the labor process, and marketed and sold the final products. The state-use scheme was identical to the state-accounts system with the exception that prison-produced products were not sold on the open market. Rather, goods and services provided by inmate labor were used within the institutions themselves or were consumed by their state agencies. Public works projects benefited from this arrangement as inmates were used in the construction of roads, railways, public buildings, and even other prisons.

In order to understand the debates of the 1880s over the varied use of these production regimes, it is essential that we understand how and why they developed, consider the conditions under which they were employed, and reveal the contradictions that undermined and changed them. In doing so, I wish to demonstrate how state managers initiated these various prison labor schemes in an attempt to balance their own administrative, fiscal and legitimation problems and how and why this extension of state power ultimately failed as public policy.

The Origins of the Prison as Factory

Laboring within the walls of America's penal institutions dates from the Colonial period.[23] The notions of "hard labor" and penal servitude were grounded in moral, legal, practical, and, as time went on, increasingly economic foundations. As a representative of the Philadelphia Society for Alleviating the Miseries of Prisons, a reformist organization rooted in Quakerism, urged before the state legislature in 1788, "solitary confinement to hard labor and a total abstinence from spirituous liquors will prove the means of reforming these unhappy creatures." "All prisons should be workhouses," they declared, as the basis for both punishment and reformation.[24]

By 1790, Pennsylvania had stipulated in its penal code that

prisoners would work in the recently erected cell house of the
Walnut Street jail. By engaging their charges in labor, jailers
could count on a more disciplined environment and the products derived from the inmate's labor would offset the cost of
confinement. At Walnut Street, prisoner accounts were debited
for the cost of clothing, upkeep, and raw materials. To
"encourage industry as evidence of reformation" their accounts
were credited with the proceeds of their labor, and, if there was
an excess over costs, they were to receive half upon their
release.[25] Few among prison officials and politicans expected a
profit from the institutions at this time; Massachusetts Warden
Bradford called his prison a "benevolent institution" deserving
of state support.[26] Prisons had few marketing links to the
outside for their products, the labor process was based on
handi-craft production, and the intended purpose of forced
labor was one of deterrence, reformation and control rather
than profit maximization. Virtually all prisons were run on
public-accounts systems.

Between 1790 and 1930, the nation's numbers more than
tripled from nearly four to almost thirteen million. By 1830,
half a million people lived in urban areas with populations
exceeding 50,000 residents.[27] In Philadelphia, the transfer of
felons from rural counties had the effect of swelling the
numbers in the Walnut Street jail and soon the moral regime of
solitary, hard labor, diet control, and hygiene was in disarray.
Eventually, conditions at the jail erupted into a political crisis
for the state legislature. Jail Inspectors had begun pardoning
prisoners to alleviate over-crowding, abuses and neglect were
exposed and serious riots took place in 1817, 1819, 1820, and
1821. In the uprising of 1820, nearly the entire prison population escaped.[28]

The result was unanimous condemnation of the Walnut
Street jail by the Philadelphia Society for Alleviating the
Miseries of Prisons, the Inspectors of the jail itself. This
denunciation was summarized in a Report of the Commissioners on the Penal Code which stated that conditions had caused
the prison of Philadelphia to ". . . forfeit the high character it
once possessed, and to become a reproach to the city in which it

was located, and to the state by whom it ought to be superintended."[29] The ideals of liberal-democratic discipline had confronted the day-to-day realities of the liberal-capitalist state. Yet rather than change directions, the state pressed on; all called for the building of new state penitentiaries. Undertaking the most ambitious public works program in Pennsylvania's history to date, the Western and Eastern facilities were erected by the laws of 1817 and 1821, marking the beginnings of Pennsylvania's prison "system" and thus a major expansion of its repressive sub-apparatus. Both institutions adopted handicraft production within cells, by law, in 1829.

The situation was similar elsewhere as other states increased their commitment to institutional punishment. Such expansion however only increased the already deficit ridden prisons. In addition to construction costs, the Philadelphia prison operated at an average annual loss of $30,000, and in New York, from 1797 till 1821, the state prison at New Gate ran an average annual loss of just under $17,000.[30] At the first New Jersey state prison at Trenton, losses in the 1820s amounted to some $3,000 to $4,000 annually. In fact, the prison cost the state $165,000 over 30 years; one-third the total state tax revenues for the period.[31] And yet change was on the horizon. With the rise of a merchant-capitalist class, the expansion of markets, and a shortage of cheap labor (prior to the massive immigration of the mid 1800s), the prison became an attractive setting for the developing industrial model. Meanwhile, prison and state officials were looking for ways of deferring rapidly increasing costs. The implications were clear. As E. B. Mittleman characterized the situation in 1921:

> [In] the late twenties and early thirties, a re-organization in the prisons took place and the modern prison system was launched . . . Instead of working them [inmates] in small shops under "mutual inspection," large shops were erected in the prison court yards where supervision and discipline were easy. "A single overseer," says the Boston Prison Discipline Society, describing the new shops at the Massachusetts prison, "really does more to prevent evil

communication between one hundred men in this shop, than ten overseers in . . . the old brick building." Instead of manufacturing on their own account, the prisoners were now let out to contractors.[32]

In 1819, three years after its construction, and by order of the state legislature, the New York penitentiary at Auburn was the first to adopt the new system of contracted, "joint labor" by day, solitary by night, along with the "lock-step" and continual silence. Auburn turned a profit by 1828. A keeper there stated "great risk and losses are avoided, and much private capital, and personal interest and enterprise, are brought into action, in promoting the active and profitable employment of the convicts."[33] Under the Auburn plan, initial construction costs were lower and more space was provided given that the cells were smaller and more austere since only nightly confinement was necessary. And the constant surveillance provided by the centralized production not only prevented "evil communication," but also ensured strict control and discipline over the labor process. This regime was embraced in many states; soon to follow were Connecticut, Ohio, Maine, New Hampshire, Michigan and Vermont. After all, state governments were actively involved in "mixed" (public/private) economic ventures in other spheres, why not in the prison? By merging the domain of state control with the interest of private capital, the state had created a unique social form; indeed, a new form of state apparatus and a reconstitution of state power.

In contrast, the Pennsylvania penitentiaries refused to adopt the new methods (although they did, on occasion, "yield to temptation," according to Harry Elmer Barnes, and engage in piece-price arrangements).[34] Dedicated to the notion that inmate labor was primarily for purposes of reformation and not profit, officials debated the ethics of prison labor. Steeped in the reformist and philanthropic philosophy of the early Quakers, the argument of some Pennsylvania officials was that the state and the society were best served when the penal apparatus produced, what Gustave de Beaumont and Alexis de Tocqueville called, the "deepest impression on the soul of the convict," rather than be concerned with what they considered short-term interests of costs.[35] For example, at the Eastern facility outside Philadelphia, Inspector Richard Vaux, argued again and again throughout his long career, his objections to the Auburn system of factory production. He stated in 1855 for example:

> The labor here, is not farmed out as in some State Penitentiaries . . . The prison authorities, by the operation of this [Auburn] plan, have a divided duty. They are bound to the contractor for the labor he exacts for his *per diem* paid for each convict. This is the most important interest. The care of, and the discipline, and the reformational influences which ought to be faithfully exerted for the benefit of the convict, as well as society, being less palpable when in contrast with revenue, it might most naturally happen that the contractor is favored to the detriment of the convict.[36]

And later:

> It is believed that the congregation of convicts during their incarceration for crime-punishment, and their sale to the highest bidder as human machinery, out of which profit is to be made, is of far greater evil to society, than society yet fully comprehends.[37]

Steadfast in their resolve, Eastern Penitentiary officials argued before their law makers the virtues of their system. In 1837 they stated:

> The Inspectors assure the Legislature, that if permitted to develop itself fully, under the fostering influence of that policy which has always been extended to it by the Legislature, that the time is not far distant, when the Penitentiary system of our State, will be regarded among the proudest monuments of the wisdom of her people.[38]

Apparently persuaded by the Inspectors' arguments (and seriously constrained by the fact that the structure of the facility did not permit congregate shops), the state continued to support and subsidize the Eastern facility. And pay they did. Year after year the institution posted deficits. As Barnes put it:

> Never in its history has the Eastern Penitentiary failed to be a burden upon both the state and counties . . . [it] was wholly comparable to the many pathetic cases in the last century where handi-craft artisans maintained a proud but losing and hopeless competition with the irresistible march of mechanical invention and labor-saving machinery. As time went on . . . the struggle became palpably disastrous in a financial sense.[39]

In New Jersey, the apparent failure of the first state prison – both in terms of its supposed deterrent capacity and its cost – prompted an investigation by a joint committee of the legislature in 1830 which concluded "with entire unanimity the building of a new prison, on the general plan of those at Auburn, New York."[40] Yet by 1833, both the legislative committee and the Governor had changed their position to support the Eastern Pennsylvania model rather than the Auburn plan. The committee, in outlining its advocacy of the Pennsylvania system of solitary confinement and labor, argued that the "great terror" known to have been "impressed upon the minds of the convict community by this Institution [and it would] hold out the most powerful repellant to the commission of crime" within the state. The committee contended that concern for profits must be held "subsidiary to the great ends of punishment" although at the same time they assured the legislature that within the Eastern facility "a convict can in six months earn his maintenance." The new state prison with solitary confinement for 150 convicts was open in 1836 at the cost of $179,429. Yet just four years later, the prison cost nearly $16,000 annually to operate. From 1841 to 1858 a piece-price contract system was installed and the debt reduced to $1,000. Actions by the Governor and the legislators in the early 1860s expanded congregate workshops and adopted the leasing of inmate labor to private contractors, thereby adopting, if not in name but in spirit, the Auburn system.

Interestingly, at Pennsylvania's Western Penitentiary, administrators were less enamored with the handi-craft, state-accounts regime of their Eastern counterparts. As early as 1836 the Inspectors, who were responsible for overseeing the industrial production of the prison, complained of the lack of efficiency of the solitary system. By the 1860s their attacks were increasingly vigorous. "Discard your cell labor," they declared, "change your separate system and adopt the congregate, and you will be able to use the muscle and skill of the prisoner much more to the advantage of the Commonwealth."[41] Conditions were ripe for the changeover as the post–Civil War era brought increased populations, an industrial depression, overcrowding, and a bleak financial picture for the prison. In 1866, the Inspectors argued that the legislature had two choices: adopt the new system or build new cells to support the solitary system. In 1873, a contract system of congregate shops with mechanized production was installed at the Western Penitentiary. Clearly, one contradiction embodied in the Pennsylvania system was the fiscal pressure it brought politicians and there can be little doubt this contributed to its unpopularity and eventual demise.

With the exception of the Eastern Penitentiary of Pennsylvania and, for a short period of time, the New Jersey system, private contractors, either under the contract, lease of piece-price regimes, dominated prison industries from roughly 1830 until after the Civil War. To this point it would seem that the vast majority of state managers had, by adopting the Auburn system, successfully intervened and responded to the potential problem of the "dangerous classes." They created social consensus by securing order and stability in society, permitted the protection of commerce in accordance with civil law and thereby ensured conditions of private production. Moreover, by forging an alliance with a segment of private capital, state managers were able to defer the financial cost of expanding the state apparatus. They had, in essence, successfully reproduced the conditions of their existence and legitimation.

Yet the situation was not without problems. As early as 1823, "free labor" had expressed its objection to the sale of prison-made goods. In that year, cabinet makers, engineering workers, and an *ad hoc* Workers Commission in New York complained of unfair competition. In 1834, trade unions forced the appointment of a special commission by the legislature of New York to investigate the problem. The workers demanded an end to the contract system. The commission offered modifications in the conditions of contracts, but would not yield the contract system, concluding that prison work had to be productive in order to offset costs.[42] Given the relatively weak political position of trade unions at this time, legislators had little incentive to restrict the contract system.

In the period after Reconstruction, more organized and powerful trade unions, and possibly more importantly, manufacturers, began a forceful attack on convict labor. The industrial depression of 1873 had thrown millions of "free" laborers out of work while markets for prison goods dried up. Union organizations such as the Knights of Labor and the Federation of Organized Trades and Labor Unions carried anti-contract motions into the political arena. In 1883 the Tennessee Coal, Iron and Railroad Company hired 1,300 convicts from the state penitentiary to force wage concessions from miners. Conditions there deteriorated and in 1891 the free miners burned down the camp freeing the prisoners. Only after a violent confrontation with the state militia was the leasing of convicts outlawed.

The system was equally denounced by those manufacturers not taking advantage of low-priced prison labor, and the doctrine of *laissez-faire* asserted. While the total value of production of prison industries had a relatively minor impact on the free market system as a whole, it had considerable effect within certain industries, e.g. boots and shoes, twine, furniture, etc. At their convention in 1878, the hatmakers' association for example voiced their objection to the dissolution of business due to the use of prison labor in private shops. Moreover, public sentiment began to turn as the despotism of private contracting took its toll on prisoners/workers. Reports of extreme cruelty, miserable working conditions, and deaths began to surface. In the state of Texas alone for example, 224 inmates died between the years 1886 and 1888. Rothman states that ". . . while some of the deaths could be explained away because Negroes ostensibly were already carrying 'the seeds of disease,' state inspectors agreed that at least some of the contractors . . . [were] 'guilty of inhumane treatment.'"[43] The "successful" alliance created by state managers was crumbling.

The "crisis" of convict labor did not go unnoticed by politicians seeking office who, according to Blake McKelvy, "had their ears to the ground in the early eighties, and they revealed some ability at *Realpolitik* if not in penological statecraft."[44] During that time, the Democrats, with aid of the labor vote, took control over influential state governments and eventually the White House. An onslaught of legislation arose restricting the "private" systems of contract labor and requiring some form of public-accounts system. While some states, like New York and Pennsylvania, were quick to modify and eventually outlaw private contracting, it persisted in other (mostly southern) states until the 1930s. Nevertheless, the shift away to direct public control was fairly dramatic.

According to the Reports of the Department of Labor, in 1885 only five states operated under exclusively public-accounts systems, and 11 partially under those systems. By 1923, the figures were 30 and 18 respectively, with the latter having some private system in place. The lease system, which accounted for 26 percent of the total value of goods ($24,271,078) in 1885 was gone completely; public-works accounts now represented 20 percent of the 1923 goods value of $73,820,125, up from one-tenth of one percent; and state-use had increased from eight percent to over 37 percent of total value.[45] Still pressured by ever increasing costs and the need for discipline in the institutions, public-accounts systems emerged as a compromise, but they were no substitute. As Howard Gill pointed out, "it should be noted that while the number of convicts employed in productive labor increased from 30,853 in 1885 to 51,779 in 1923, or 70 percent, the number engaged in prison duties, sick, and idle, increased from 11,024 to 32,962 or 199 percent . . . It

appears that idleness increases as public control increases."[46]
Indeed, state-use and public-accounts systems were failures at
generating revenue.

   In his survey of prison industries covering the late 1920s,
Robinson concluded that, "It is plain that the great majority of
American prisons not only fail to meet operating costs but
require heavy annual appropriations."[47] By 1929, the passage of
the Hawes-Cooper Act, a congressional bill lobbied by the
Garment Manufacturers' Association, severely restricted the
inter-state flow of prison goods by subjecting their sale to the
laws of the state in which they were sold. After its passage, state
after state enacted legislation prohibiting the sale of convict-
produced goods from other states. With the onset of the
depression, and millions outside the penitentiaries unemployed,
the issue of prison labor disappeared from the national agenda.

Discipline, Punishment, and Capitalism

Private contractors, either under the contract, lease or piece-
price systems, dominated prison industries from roughly 1830
to the immediate post-Civil War. The Auburn-style penitentiary, with its lock-step, silence, and communal labor had
become *the* model of the American prison regime. Was it for its
superior penological advantages that this system rose to such
eminence? Few could argue on these grounds. No, the advantage of the Auburn system was in how well it meshed with the
emerging industrial order of factory production, which could
be easily reproduced within the institution. As Michael Hindus
observes in his study of the Massachusetts system, "It can
hardly be a coincidence that the years in which the Auburn
system was most rigorously applied in Massachusetts were also
the years that, according to the prison's own accounting,
produced the greatest profit."[48]

   Why was it then that the prison came to resemble the factory;
whose interests did this resemblance serve, and why did the

practice ultimately fail? Was the "real" intention the production of proletarians as some revisionists contend? I would argue that there are considerable problems with this point of view which is narrowed by instrumentalism and functionalism. Who, for example, is the historical agent in this account? The "bourgeoisie?" If so, why did manufacturers join the fight against prison labor? If discipline were the only concern, why had not the Pennsylvania system survived or for that matter the treadmill? To assume that the essential role of the prison was the disciplining of the working-class is to characterize the institution as a tool placed squarely in the hands of an united class with a definable agenda at hand. Moreover, to make such an assumption also places the state in an equally instrumental position and thereby denies the institutional self-interest of the state, and neglects to consider the ways in which such self-interest shapes public policy.

My contention is that the nineteenth-century American penitentiary *did* contain a goal of economic utility and that goal reflected the interest of state managers attempting to reproduce their position within the political structure. Thus, the prison came to resemble the factory, quite literally, because it was in the interest of state officials to extend the power of the state by creating a cooperative alliance with a segment of private capital. Such "mixed" economic forms were a common practice of the early Accumulative State form. By creating this alliance, the state could, via its apparatus, accomplish its principal objectives of social consensus by confronting illegitimate behavior and establishing order and stability. This, in turn, ensured general conditions of economic production (even within the prison walls itself) and social integration by guaranteeing both collective security and the creation of social wealth. All these objectives helped to ensure the political legitimacy and material power of the liberal-capitalist state. Thus, the state had the incentive to make prison labor as profitable as possible and, given the economic developments outside the prison, it had an interest in uniting private capital and its prison populations. In this case, politics at the level of state intersected with the politics of production.

Yet through this intersection a number of unintended consequences emerged and these contradictions brought about the demise of viable prison industries. First, at the level of the apparatus, the state linked the prison to the economic movements of capitalism outside the prison doors and, once so linked, it changed the character and the mission of the institution. For the majority of prison administrators, profitable regimes met their short-term goals of both discipline and managerial efficiency of the state apparatus. Thus, one consequence of this movement was the dominance of economic activity in shaping both policy and life in the institution. As a critical report of the Eastern Penitentiary characterized the move, "Congregate labor with power-driven machinery converts prisons that should be places of punishment and reflection into factories for profit." Indeed, the prison had become the "prison/factory."

A second consequence of transforming the prison into a factory was that, as a productive concern, it was drawn into the contradictions inherent in liberal-capitalist economies. Boom and bust business cycles left stockpiled goods unsold, while markets for particular products dried up. Since changes in shift work and "layoffs" were problematic, production went on regardless of outside market conditions. Moreover, the prisons had to compete with capitalists on the outside who were constantly introducing new machinery and methods to reduce labor costs or improve products. Not only was it difficult for prison industries to adjust to such changes, but the idea of introducing "labor saving" technologies into a prison reflected the flawed logic of the state prison as an unorthodox economic form.

Finally, and most importantly, prison/factory regimes were initiated during a period of general acceptance of public/private "mixed" enterprise; a trade mark of the Accumulative State. Yet such enterprises were later viewed as trespassing the boundaries between the state and civil society as that threshold was defined in the later half of the nineteenth century. While the state had little to do with the actual operation under "privatized" contract systems (a considerable advantage to the state), the prison plant and, hence, the private contractor, benefited from cheap or free labor, as well as subsidized overhead costs since these expenditures were derived from taxes rather than private capital. By providing such subsidies, the state was directly involved in organizing a production apparatus which was competing with free industry and labor. In the case of public systems, a purely state financed and run organization was in complete violation of both the "fair" rules of *laissez-faire* liberal-capitalism, the reigning political ideology of the period. As Inspector Vaux stated of the situation in 1880:

> . . . an individual commits crime, is convicted, his physical capacity to toil is sold to a contractor who becomes a partner with the State in the manufacture of certain products, and from the sale of these products the State gets part of the profit, the contractor gets part of the profit; while the outside free laborer is paid as low a price for his free time and capacity, as his employer can afford, to come into competition with the State as a manufacturer. This is called punishment of the convict for his crime.[49]

In sum, when faced with rising prison populations and mounting deficits during the 1820s, the majority of state governments turned to private capital to make prisons viable economic units. They had neither the tax base to support expanding prison systems nor the incentive to raise taxes. During this period, "mixed" enterprises were not uncommon and the political weakness of unorganized "free" labor permitted the state to initiate and subsidize production within the walls of prisons. This movement was justified, ideologically, by a historically-grounded notion that prisoners should work for their reformation, punishment and keep. The movement contributed to a half century of a politically and economically "convenient" use of institutionalization of the criminal element of society.

By the 1880s however, working-class resistance and organized capital had united with a reformist critique of abuses under the private system to create a new crisis of legitimation for state governments. In order to alleviate this crisis, reformist-oriented states first took control of production away from private capital and set up state-account and state-use systems in an attempt to appease criticism while continuing to off-set the cost of the penal apparatus. These systems however, failed to be economically viable and by the 1930s, with the onset of economic crisis, states were forced to contend with prisons holding idle and unproductive populations.

There can be no doubt that the prison was a disciplinary apparatus or, as Jeremy Bentham characterized it in 1792, "A mill for grinding rogues honest, and idle men industrious." Teaching recalcitrant citizens the ways of thrift and labor was also in the interest of the state, since a "successful" reformation of the prisoner meant a reintegration into market/exchange relations upon release and the assurance of social consensus. Thus the "power to punish" was not so much directed by and solely in the interest of a particular class, but rather was in the collective interest of all members of a class society reproduced through capitalist production.

In existence for more than 50 years, it can hardly be a coincidence that with the decline of economically productive prison industries, state and prison authorities began to expand the use of parole as a way of reducing prison populations. While Rothman would have us believe that developments in parole were due to the ideological agenda of Progressive reformers, Sheldon Messinger and his colleagues contend that, at least in California, it was prison over-crowding that prompted parole expansion at this time, rather than any rehabilitative movement.[50] Clearly, the theoretical model of the state being employed here suggests that, while an over-crowded prison is problematic, a prison that is both unproductive *and* over-crowded is cause for alarm.

Working to Reproduce the State

The history of public social control facilities during the

nineteenth and early twentieth centuries is littered with attempts by the state, some more successful than others, to use inmate labor to reproduce the state apparatus. The experience of the juvenile reformatory, for example, was not unlike that of the prison. In the early years of the "House of Refuge," the bulk of the inmate's day revolved around labor whether in New York, Philadelphia, Boston or Providence. Various arrangements existed as to the system of production, including private contracting of child labor and state sale of products. By the 1870s, the contract system dominated. In Illinois, for example, immediately following the opening of the State Reform School at Pontiac in 1871, administrators made arrangements with various Chicago firms to lease the labor of inmates. This program was said to constitute the institution's "educational" component.[51]

The contracting of children ended along with the existence of "privatized" production regimes in America's prisons. The practice was swept away by the specific campaign of opposition by free labor and manufacturers and by the more general movement to limit the exploitation of children by capital. In 1871, labor groups called on the state legislature to end its substantial appropriations to the New York House of Refuge because the use of child labor had permitted a private contractor a profit of $183,000.[52] The practice continued, however, due to the support of contractors and institutional authorities. Later, a Report by the Board of Charities in 1879 was highly critical of the treatment of children by private contractors, stating that "It subordinates the reformation and improvement of the child to the interest of the contractor; introduces a foreign element into the institution in the person of the contractors employ'es [sic], who have no sympathy with the cause of reform, but, on the contrary, exercise a vicious influence."[53] By 1884, opposition to the practice had overwhelmed state authorities which then outlawed private contracting in all juvenile facilities, while two years later, the state enacted its first child labor legislation.

While private capital was being removed from the direct exploitation of inmates within social control facilities, the state continued its attempts to "train" inmates and to use the power of the state to "guide" them into wage labor upon release. One particularly striking and relatively successful attempt occurred in New York at the Western House of Refuge for women at Albion which opened in 1894 and was operational till 1931. Here, where women between the ages of 15 and 30 were sentenced for promiscuous activities, vagrancy, and the like, the state engaged in what Nicole Hahn Rafter calls "sexual control and vocational control" of working-class women.[54] That is, by incarcerating these women, the state attempted to control the inmates' sexuality by "training 'loose' young women to accept middle-class standards of propriety." But beyond appeasing the moral concerns of middle-class women reformers, and more specific to the concerns here, the state was also interested in attempting to halt the "unproductive" aspects of their life-styles and the possibility of their bearing children and becoming state dependents. The state extended vocational control by vigorously training these women in the tasks and role of home-maker with the intention of their engaging in "productive" activities upon their release, either as non-paid wives in the homes of their own families or as wage labor in others. According to Rafter, one quarter of the women were paroled directly into live-in domestic positions, and of the 50 percent paroled to their own families, a "sizable proportion" also took jobs as domestics.

The House of Refuge in Albion remains an exception for the period, however, as an efficient state organization for transforming recalcitrant citizens into "republican machines." In most cases where "training" and "rehabilitation" activities were attempted, few were so successful. However, such programs did provide a valuable function for institutional authorities and state legislatures: they provided for orderly and controlled facilities and contributed to reducing costs. If products could not be sold on the open market then inmate labor was used, on a daily basis, to reproduce the state apparatus. For what was called "occupational therapy," "vocational training" and the like, functioned as institutional subsistence and maintenance.

In the adult penitentiaries, for example, when private capital was driven from its walls as we saw above, prison "industries" had evolved, by the end of the period, into the production of clothing, shoes, bedding, and agricultural produce for the institution itself. If products were consumed outside the institution it was on strictly state-use accounts. William Slingerland, a child welfare researcher of the day, summarizes the trend in juvenile training schools during the progressive period:

> Most of the large institutions have what they call trades departments, and use them mainly for repair and construction work about the plants. The inmates become the unskilled helpers of the carpenters, painters . . . farmers, and dairymen. A majority of the tailor shops are devoted to the mending of worn garments; most of the shoe shops are used for the cobbling of impaired shoes. This gives a small amount of instruction while utilizing the labor of inmates in reducing the expense of the institution.[55]

Even more dramatic was the use of inmate labor in mental hospitals. The tradition of patient labor in America's early mental hospitals is revealed in the records of the Bloomingdale Asylum of New York. Originally undertaken as part of "enlightened" principles in the care of the mentally ill at the close of the eighteenth century, an essential component of "moral treatment" was the employment of patients – at times, whether they liked it or not. As William Russell recounts, for Polly P., age 31, admitted to the Asylum in April 1823 for example,

> it was recorded that the attending physician "demanded employment of her or deprivation of food and forcible exhibition of medicines and blisters." She had ideas of imaginary wealth, a spirit of pride and independence, despising employment. "She at first chose scanty food – but medicine and blisters caused her to choose knitting, sewing, spinning and quilting – ordinary diet whenever she would work. But bread and water when she would not." She was discharged in November 1823, "with habits of industry."[56]

As early as 1833, the hospital director proposed that the bulk of the hired help who maintained the garden and farm be dismissed and replaced with patients. By 1850, the newest director, Dr Earle, argued that "better results" could be obtained if the patients "could be subjected to continuous and systematic bodily and mental training by persons fully competent for such duty."[57]

While such a rigorous "scheme of manual labor" would not appear at Bloomingdale until after the turn of the century, inmates in the mid-nineteenth century were pressed into daily maintenance. Over 50 percent of the women and 40 percent of the men were said to be engaged in "much voluntary assistance in the care of the halls, in the making of beds and washing of dishes, etc."[58] The practice of engaging patients in labor was as prevalent at other hospitals, including the Worcester and Utica Asylums where superintendents proudly exalted in the efficiency of their operations. As Rothman put it, "The well-ordered asylum was a hard-working asylum."[59]

As time went on, "occupational therapy" replaced "moral treatment." While the chores remained the same, more extensive production took place. At Bloomingdale, the new century brought formal workshops where patients performed joinery, basketry, rug making, brass and leather work, and chair caneing. A print shop produced thousands of pieces of printed matter and bound books and magazines. While Gerald Grob contends that, "Although patient labor had some minor impact on institutional finances, economic considerations played a decidedly minor role,"[60] Rothman declares that

> Occupational therapy, however, was more than an occasional patient weaving or joining the wheelbarrow brigade. As in correctional institutions, it affected the very existence of the mental hospital, for inmate labor was essential to the day-to-day maintenance of the facility. And there was no disputing this fact. Superintendents' reports frankly conceded that without patients working, costs would have been dramatically higher, perhaps even

so high as to discourage public reliance upon institutional care.[61]

Willard State Hospital in New York ran its entire boot and shoe industry, which had supplied 2,500 patients for years, with just two employees. In addition, the hospital provided its own milk and produce as well as thousands of towels, pillowcases, sheets and mattresses, which, according to its manager, translated into a savings of "many thousands of dollars" for New York State. Similar data exist from other New York Hospitals as well as those in Massachusetts, Illinois, and Virginia. "Call a facility a hospital," Rothman concludes, "use the rhetoric of the mental hygiene movement, but ultimately know that the institution was in the asylum business."[62]

Despite some successes, the state's attempt to utilize institutions to transform their problem citizens through "vocational training" and the like was circumvented by a number of unintended consequences. These contradictions were located within the structuration of the state apparatus itself. Thus, internal labor, put in place as part of a rehabilitative or therapeutic regime, was exploited by facility administrators with their own agenda. Their day-to-day interests were in running orderly, cost-effective institutions and thus reproducing the state apparatus and their place within it. This self-interest created the absurd situation whereby individuals who were most likely candidates for release were those whose labor was most needed by the institution, and were thus more likely to remain.[63]

Secondly, attempts to train individuals failed because the state, excluded from ordering private production, could not accurately gauge the needs of the oscillating labor market. Thus, the state often trained individuals in jobs that did not exist outside of the institution – a chronic problem of prison labor. The obverse situation accounts, in part, for the limited success of the New York Refuge for women discussed above which had direct linkages, through middle-class reformers, to placing women as domestics (a relatively stable labor market) in private homes. Even when these kinds of problems became apparent over time, policies persisted because they contributed to easing the immediate problem of the fiscal burden of institutional social control; an issue always at the forefront of the concerns of state legislators.

3

Public Welfare in an Age of Social and Economic Crises

A historiography of public welfare policy during the nineteenth and early twentieth centuries reveals the considerable challenge faced by local and state governments in confronting a population of people who could not, or would not, participate in wage labor. This challenge was rooted in the tension between the often conflicting goals and priorities of the liberal-capitalist state: a state often at odds with itself; indeed an ambivalent state. On the one hand, by the early 1800s, Americans had inherited a history and culture which supported the idea that, as Secretary of New York Yates stated in 1824, "the total want of a pauper system, would be inconsistent, with a humane, liberal, and enlightened policy."[1] And yet, on the other hand, as a Massachusetts Legislative committee argued in 1833, "As Government was instituted for the security of life, liberty and poverty of the subject, as neither property nor life are safe, while the idle and able-bodied may without restraint demand support from the industrious and the thrifty, it is therefore the duty of the Government to protect the last class against the unjust demands and incursions of the first."[2] The principal solution offered to reconcile this dilemma was the poorhouse and thus, any history of American public welfare during this time is, in part, a history of this sub-apparatus of the state.

Poverty, Dependency, and the Poorhouse

The poorhouse was not a new idea when America began using them. Principally an English creation, the first of its kind in the Colonies, in Boston, admitted inmates on December 26, 1664. By the close of the Colonial period, most large towns had established an almshouse, although it was still considered an "experiment" at the turn of the nineteenth century.[3] Yet by 1850, the almshouse emerged as the dominant response to the sick, the insane, orphaned children, vagrants, the able-bodied poor and the like. What I want to argue here is that this ascendancy was the result of the failure of the older laws and methods of relief to confront the changing realities of nineteenth-century political and economic life. The alternative, non-institutional practices of the past, would become, in the view of local and state level officials and the public, ineffectual and even counter-productive. But more than the practices themselves, contention focused on the laws surrounding the legal claim to town alms; the establishment of "settlement." Having their own origins in seventeenth-century Elizabethan legislation, these statutes were hard pressed to cope with the massive social and economic changes ushered in during the Jacksonian period. First, let us consider the traditional methods of poor relief and uncover the circumstances and contradictions which were undermining their use.

Despite the existence of the almshouse, the majority of poor had customarily been disposed of by somewhat less formal means. Those close to the center of town life might stay in their homes (a practice known as outdoor relief) or were placed with relatives, friends, or fellow church members with aid of alms. For others, the practices of boarding-out served local townships well. The boarding of a pauper often involved calling on townsfolk, a widow for example, and negotiating a price for their role as keeper. The evidence indicates that during the mid-eighteenth century, people of all social standings were willing to take on this role, although the majority were probably "middle-class."[4] This method was economical, needed little supervision or attention, and served to integrate the local poor into the structure of rural social life. Under the boarding-out system, not only did the indigent live in private dwellings, but the practice permitted and encouraged all community members to participate in support of the poor. "No separation between the dependent poor persons and the community appeared. Indeed, the rural community as a whole was actively involved in the system of poor relief."[5] Yet, between the revolution and about 1825, these apparently flexible and informal arrangements began to break down under the weight of social and economic change. First, expanded commercial activity – particularly in the Northern urban areas of New York, Boston, Philadelphia, and Baltimore – had the effect of drawing in previously isolated, rural communities into the city spheres. This rapid growth "reflected the development of a local consuming market. There was an increased demand for foodstuffs for this urban population, with a consequent widening of the market areas around these urban areas . . ."[6] Local governments expanded transportation links to move excess agricultural production, cattle, and light manufacturing products to urban markets. The effect of this transformation in the New York area is summarized by Robert Cray this way:

> If closer ties to Manhattan gave farmers a ready market for their surpluses, it also showed them to feel the effects of economic depressions more readily; if ferry service and roads facilitated travel, it also gave transients better access to the rural hinterland. The commercial farming regions . . . also witnessed the development of a more stratified social structure with fewer opportunities for advancement and, not surprisingly, the growth of a landless laboring class . . . Moreover, the close-knit social fabric of village life started to give way to a more individual oriented society caught in the process of economic development.[7]

The erosion of social cohesion, the attraction of wealth, and the increasing stratification of towns and villages had specific consequences for traditional poor relief practice. Townsfolk, particularly those of the middle and upper classes, became less willing to take in and board the increasing number of strangers and outsiders appearing in their area.[8] Those that were willing were demanding greater compensation for the role as keeper, adding to the rising costs of poor relief.

One result was that local communities began to turn to more formal methods of treating the poor. These included the pauper auction, the almshouse and increasingly, the evocation of settlement laws permitting the removal of the "undeserving" poor. The auction, a more stigmatizing public ritual, did away with those on the margins of village life at the lowest possible price and provided cheap labor for those willing to take them on. This practice seemed to retain the advantages of informal arrangements while, at the same time, it imposed a more punitive treatment and kept a check on costs. Informal methods were more dramatically pushed aside with the adoption of the almshouse, still however, a relatively rare turn prior to 1820. The principal advantages of the poorhouse seem clear. It would isolate the dependent from the growing, middle-class community who increasingly considered the pauper an idler and profligate. Rather than have the indigent scattered around town in private dwellings, or worse yet, begging on street corners, the almshouse centralized their relief administration and provided for more effective surveillance of their activities by one overseer. It was said that the institution would protect the dependent from possible despotism of private keepers and treat all the poor in equal fashion. Indeed, in this sense the poorhouse, like the penitentiary, was a truly democratic institution. And finally, and as some argued most importantly, the facility would – despite the initial cost of construction – reduce poor relief expenditures.

Last but not least, in an effort to confront the influx of strangers and the cost supporting the poor, many local officials vigorously enforced the laws which sought to determine if a person was "settled" in their community. Settlement laws, having their origins in Elizabethan legislation, placed responsibility for the poor in the hands of local authorities and used taxation to support such care. The underlying assumption of local responsibility was in the idea of a *quid pro quo*. If a person worked in, owned property, and paid taxes in a local community then the government of that community was responsible for the maintenance of that individual if they should be "reduced to want." The determination of such responsibility was fixed according to a variety of often confusing local statutes governing the right acquired by a person to claim aid or relief under the poor laws. In some localities, the poor, or even those having the potential of becoming dependents, were "warned off" by authorities before they became settled. Others were ordered removed from the community if it was determined their settlement lay elsewhere. Still others would be supported by a town even though they had not gained settlement (e.g. because the individual was too frail to be moved). The supporting jurisdiction, however, had the right to sue the community of origin in order to recover the cost of relief. It follows that settlement laws were a mechanism of the local state legal sub-apparatus. They were intended to reinforce the legitimacy of the local state as a responsive body within the *quid pro quo* arrangement and, at the same time, protect local citizens from undue financial responsibility.

By the turn of the century then, poor relief in America was a myriad of localized laws and practices set up to deal with the particular needs of individual communities. Yet within the next two decades, existing poor relief practice would be undermined by both its own contradictions and events beyond its control. Given the changes in the structure of social life outlined above, the practice of boarding-out was now little more than an auction without ceremony. In both cases, the poor were sold off to people, many of them nearly as destitute as the paupers themselves, who forced them to labor with little care and provision. Moreover, despite the auction, these practices were increasingly regarded as costly and inefficient. Likewise, the notion of in-home relief was rapidly being considered part of the problem rather than the solution. Critics simply cited the English experience as evidence of the obvious failure of this practice.

Yet arguably, the most problematic issue centered on the mounting litigation involved in appeals and suits over the determination of settlement, and the maintenance and removal of the poor. Communities found themselves spending more to litigate settlement disputes and appeals than they had ever spent on poor relief. As one analyst concluded of the situation in New York:

> approximately 1,796 individuals were removed in the state in 1822 at a cost of more than $25,000, which was estimated to be sufficient to have supported 2,383 poor persons for a year. Disputes involving settlements resulted in one hundred and twenty-seven appeals to the court, cost – $13,500, which might have provided adequately for the care of 450 dependent persons.[9]

Settlement laws, originally evoked as a mechanism of social and fiscal control by the local state, had the contradictory effect of undermining these very goals. The evolving legal sub-apparatus of the state – embodied in justices, overseers, lawyers and constables – had used the laws to expand its own control and authority, ultimately circumventing the original purpose of the laws. Moreover, the appeals process demonstrated how legal provisions, intended to secure the consensus and integration functions of the state, may be exploited by all social groups – even the subordinate classes – to advance their respective interests.

Finally, two events in the early nineteenth century seriously challenged the ability of prevailing poor relief systems to cope and engendered the movement toward institutional policies. The first was the Embargo Act of 1807 which prohibited American ships from sailing to foreign parts. The action was an attempt by Jefferson to coerce England and France to end shipping blockades that were threatening US interests. Rather than punishing these powers however, the Embargo had a devastating impact on America's economy.[10] The economic "ripple effect" from the port cities to the rural areas, particularly in New England, was dramatic. As a consequence, poor relief expenditures in towns and cities rose dramatically. Rates in New York City nearly doubled between 1807 and 1809 and overcrowding in the city's poorhouse prompted the erection of an additional facility at Bellvue in 1811. Surrounding communities opened or reopened their own institutions for the poor.[11] The second event was the so called Panic of 1819. Following an expansion boom between 1815 and 1818, a collapse in prices created economic chaos, bankruptcy, and unemployment. Again, the effectiveness of poor relief efforts was severely tested and found wanting. Yet scorn was directed not at the effects of economic uncertainty, but rather at the "depraved and vicious" character of the pauper.

The crisis of poor relief induced two leading states, Massachusetts and New York, to initiate legislative inquiries and to produce reports on the subject. In Massachusetts, the paper was submitted by Josiah Quincy, Chairman of the investigative committee, in 1821. Entitled the "Report of the Committee on the Pauper Laws of this Commonwealth," the document reported the result of a survey of paupers provisions in Massachusetts towns. While the committee was burdened with an inadequate response rate, they nevertheless made conclusions based on the returns of 162 jurisdictions with a total population of 287,437 and 4,340 paupers. The committee estimated that there were no fewer than 7,000 paupers in the entire state supported at an annual rate of more than $350,000. The committee was critical of at-home relief stating that, out of all modes of treating the poor, this practice had proved to be "the most wasteful, the most expensive, and the most injurious to their morals and destructive of their industrious habits." The report (and the majority of the "Returns from the Towns") favored almshouses having the character of workhouses "as the most economical mode" where work, primarily agricultural, would be provided and where dependents would be supervised under a Board of Overseers. Like most statements of the day concerning the origins of poverty, the Committee blamed intemperance as *the* most powerful and universal cause of pauperism.[12]

In New York, Secretary of State Yates delivered his report in

1824 after surveying the state's poor law districts and their
practices. Yates estimated the total number of poor in New
York to be 22,111 at a cost, in 1822, of close to $500,000. Like
the Quincy Committee of Massachusetts, the Yates report
advocated the establishment of a system of county poorhouses
modelled after the "House of Industry" which had been erected
in Rensselaer county in 1820. The idea was that each inmate
would work to his or her own ability as a means of stimulating
industry and sharing the expense of their maintenance. These
houses of employment would ideally be connected to a workhouse or penitentiary "for the reception and discipline of sturdy
beggars and vagrants." Street beggary would be entirely
prohibited.[13] The Committee called for the abolishment of all
orders of removal and appeals and stated that persons who
claimed relief should receive it in the county where they became
sick or infirm, while the expense of erecting poorhouses should
be paid by the counties and raised by taxes through four annual
instalments.

The bulk of the recommendations contained in the Yates
report were adopted by the legislature later on that year. The
state required the counties to erect one or more poorhouses and
to appoint county relief officials who were to manage the
houses. By 1835, 51 out of 54 state counties had almshouses and
by 1838 the amount the overseers provided for indoor relief was
double that of outdoor. By the close of the 1830s, the population receiving outdoor relief in the state had nearly doubled to
8,225; by 1850 it was nearly 10,000.[14] Similarly in Massachusetts, at the time of Quincy's report, the state had some 85
almshouses; 15 years later 180 were reported, and by mid-
century, the number had reached 204.[15] The example of these
leading states followed throughout the country as legislatures
either passed new laws or revised old ones which, while not
necessarily requiring the construction of a poorhouse, strongly
encouraged the establishment of the institutions.[16] While there
was of course opposition to the movement – either on the
grounds that the state was trampling over local communities or
that the initial costs were prohibitive for sparsely populated
rural counties – it was no match for the apparent fiscal,

administrative, and "moral" advantages of the institution. Throughout America, the almshouse became the symbol of poor relief.

While of course most communities had a "choice" of how they would relieve their poor, there was a fundamental quality to the poorhouse which was hard to resist. It swept the streets of vagrants and beggars, removing them from the eyes and minds of the public, while stigmatizing the able-bodied for their idleness. At the same time, the state appeared to fulfill its benevolent role for the helpless dependent. Moreover, those advocating the advantages of the almshouse to towns and state legislatures in the 1820s, cited first its financial benefits in light of available alternatives. Given its precisely miserable conditions, the poorhouse was intended as a "last resort" for poverty and dependency, thereby ensuring a rough distinction between the "deserving" and "undeserving" poor. By providing a level of subsistence just below the alternative of wage labor, the state could insure that as many citizens as possible had little choice but to participate in labor markets which in turn, had the effect of reducing (or at least not inflating) wage levels. This, in essence, was the mechanism that the reformers and advocates of the poorhouse argued would "stimulate industry and orderly and regular habits." "Reformation" was not located on any real agenda or program, rather, the facility itself would terrorize the poor into any independent wage labor, at any price, when faced with the alternatives of incarceration or starvation. In fact, many communities reported that when a house was constructed, poor rates immediately fell off.

Few options to the poorhouse for the able-bodied were feasible, from the position of the state, in a developing capitalist society at this time. Outdoor relief, while always present (and, out of necessity, used more extensively later), had to be discouraged. Not only was it more expensive than the poorhouse but by providing such relatively non-stigmatizing relief, the state would violate the spirit of the original poor laws and the individualistic ideology of Social Darwinism. At home relief would remove the "last resort" character of the poorhouse and thus blur the distinction between deserving and undeserving poor, producing both middle-class, as well as working-class antagonism to such "freeloading."[17] As the first principle of the Quincy Report had stated, "That of all modes of providing for the poor, the most wasteful, the most expensive, and the most injurious to their morals and destructive of their industrious habits is that of supply in their own families."[18]

From a state-centered view, the evidence from Massachusetts, New York, and other states suggests that the accelerated adoption of the almshouse was a direct result of action taken at the level of state government. This tier of the state had the constitutional power to play a coordinating role in imposing an administrative order on the chaotic and ineffectual results of localized practices which threatened to undermine the functions of government. And yet, imposing such uniformity eroded the *quid pro quo* arrangement of local responsibility. By modifying restrictive settlement and removal laws, the upper-tiered administrative units of the state had to take more responsibility for the cost of supporting the poor. That was the bargain. Legislatures could hardly expect local communities to support strangers who, in the eyes of local officials, had never contributed anything to their town. Thus the distinction between "settled" and "unsettled" poor was beginning to break down and county or state almshouses/farms, and the network of "Houses of Correction" were the institutional mechanisms by which the states took control, and with it the expense, of the relief and control of the poor.

From "Houses of Industry" to "Disgraceful Memorials"

However, before long, the "new" system of county indoor relief was itself in crisis. For what was hailed as the final solution to dependency revealed itself as yet another administrative, jurisdictional, and financial mess. In New York, annual reports from throughout the state to the legislature uncovered shocking abuse of inmates. Idleness was pervasive, especially in the larger houses. Economic depressions between 1837 and 1843, and later between 1857 and 1858, combined with the dramatic increase in immigration, placed an incredible burden on relief agencies. The cost of both indoor and outdoor relief had expanded and considerable controversy surrounded the disbursement of temporary relief.

By mid-century, reformers such as Dorothea Dix, through groups such as the New York Association for Improving the Conditions of the Poor, criticized the situation of the "mixed" almshouse. The jobless demanded the "right to work" and the "right to relief," and all looked to state governments to provide an answer. In state after state, investigative bodies, appointed by legislatures, chronicled the failure of current relief practices, both financially and practically. In New York, a select committee of the senate concluded most dramatically – after spending five months during 1856 investigating the conditions of the states' almshouses – that

> the great mass of the poor-houses they have inspected, are the most disgraceful memorials of the public charity . . . The evidence taken by the committee exhibits such a filth, nakedness, licentiousness, general bad morals, and disregard for religion and the common religious observances, as well as of gross neglect of the most ordinary comforts and decencies of life, as if published in detail would disgrace the state and shock humanity.[19]

Massachusetts was the first to create a state board of charities in 1863 following legislative committee recommendations that a central agency was needed to coordinate the activities of the system of public charities. As Governor Fenton of New York stated in his address to the legislature in 1867:

> For some years past the State has made large annual appropriations to aid in the support of Orphan Asylums, Hospitals, Homes for the Friendless and other charitable institutions. No adequate provision, however, has been

made by law for the inspection of these and other corporations of a like character . . .

There are a great number of these institutions, and the
amount contributed to their support by public authorities,
and by public benevolence is large, and so many persons –
the aged, the helpless, the infirm and the young – fall
under their care, that I deem it expedient that the State
should exercise a reasonable degree of supervision over
them.[20]

State government were grappling to gain some rational control
over the system and expenditures. Later that year New York
established its Board. By 1873 Boards were set up in Illinois,
Pennsylvania, North Carolina, Rhode Island, Michigan, Wisconsin, Kansas, and Connecticut.

Interested in curbing the growth of dependency, the state
board of New York appointed Dr Charles Hoyt, the board's
first secretary, to investigate its causes. Hoyt visited all 64
public almshouses in the state, surveying 12,614 inmates, and
submitted his report entitled "The Causes of Pauperism" in
1876. Hoyt stated that

Most cases of pauperism are due to idleness, improvi-
dence, drunkenness, or other forms of vicious indulgence,
which are frequently, if not universally, heredity in character . . . To keep such families together is contrary to
sound policy; the sooner they can be separated and broken
up the better it will be for the children and society at large.
Vigorous efforts must be instituted to break the line of
pauper descent.

He went on to criticize outdoor relief, stating that

When persons, naturally idle and improvident, have experienced for a few months the convenience of existing
upon the labor of others, they are very likely to resort to
this means of living as often and as continuously as
possible . . . Still another evil that has contributed to the

increase of paupers is the absence of employment for the
inmates of the poorhouses . . . Suitable labor on the other
hand, would make them conscious of their own power,
which they would be unwilling to waste, and which
would impel them to leave at the earliest moment. Hard
labor is especially necessary for the many vagabonds who
drift into public poorhouses, particularly in the winter
months.[21]

Hoyt's report became the definitive statement on the nature of
poverty and dependence in America during the period. And
yet, how was "hard labor" going to reform inmates when, by
his own account, one-third of the almshouse inmates were
mentally ill in addition to those who were physically incapable
of labor? Michael Katz contends that Hoyt manipulated his
findings in order to fabricate a hereditary-based vision of
poverty when, in fact, many young, able-bodied, working-
class poor inhabited the almshouse during cycles of employment and destitution.[22] Yet Hoyt never mentions the severe
depression the country was enduring throughout the period of
his investigation.

Hoyt's report contributed to a heightened criticism of outdoor relief and "the enormous and growing evils arising from
this lavish and generally indiscriminate distribution of public
beneficence." The system, critics contended, was awash in
political corruption and waste.[23] In Kings county New York in
1877 more than 46,000 (8 percent of the county population) had
received $141,207 – a record expenditure. The Bureau of
Charities, organized in New York under private auspices and at
the forefront of the "charity organization movement," firmly
took the position that such public expenditures for outdoor
relief was to be avoided and that any such relief should be given
only under cases of extreme hardship and exclusively through
private agencies. With the help of the Bureau, New York City
and Kings county succeeded in completely abolishing public
outdoor relief in the form of cash between July 1874 and
January 1875. In their annual report of 1875, the commissioners
of the city department of charities noted that despite suspending

outdoor relief, they had been able to reduce the poorhouse population. They pointed out, with amazing frankness, that

> Care has been taken not to diminish the terrors of this last resort of poverty, because it has been deemed better that a few should test the minimum rate at which existence can be preserved, than that many should find the poorhouse so comfortable a home that they would brave the shame of pauperism to gain admission to it.[24]

Indeed, the relationship between the almshouse and outdoor relief was a delicate one for public officials. On the one hand, there had to be considerable stigma attached to residence in the almshouse, and its conditions had to be bleak enough as not to encourage the marginal poor to seek admission. On the other hand, as Alexander Johnson, the General Secretary of the Nation Conference on Charities and Correction would state in 1911:

> When ... the institution is known to be so bare of comfort, so severe in its discipline, or so badly managed, that public opinion will not sanction a decent old person being forced into it, then outdoor relief inevitably increases in amount, and so with its increase comes a rapid growth in the amount of general pauperism. A well-managed, comfortable almshouse is a preventive of unnecessary pauperism. Those who really need public care can have it there, and those who do not need it will not seek it there.[25]

By the spring of 1893, depression once again racked the country. In the year 1894, unemployment rose to over 18 percent of the civilian labor force.[26] Organized "industrial armies" of the unemployed demanded federal relief and public works programs, adopting the cry of "employment rather than charity." Again, treatment of the able-bodied unemployed became the center of public controversy, and again states acted to restrict public outdoor relief, although many local overseers who had the authority to distribute temporary outdoor relief did so since there were few alternatives to cope with the volume and character of public dependency at this time. Thus, despite attempts to restrict it, poor relief expenditures rose throughout the states. In New York, cities and counties requested increased appropriations from the legislature as many had spent well over budgeted amounts.

The desperate nature of the problem of able-bodied unemployment in the 1890s prompted the creation of public and private work-relief projects in which participants were required to perform a certain amount of manual labor as a prerequisite for relief. The labor test, which was to sift the "deserving" from "undeserving" poor, usually consisted of wood cutting, ditch-digging or stone breaking for men and sewing and laundering for women. New York City, with funds appropriated from the state, initiated a $1,000,000 parks improvement project while others were put to work cleaning streets and whitewashing tenements. Finally, many were furnished with supplies to begin "farming" vacant city lots to grow their own subsistence.[27]

During the depression of 1907–8, the "tramp" problem, as it was referred to, again faced public officials. Roaming vagrants and able-bodied homeless appeared throughout America's towns and cities. In New York, welfare administrators desperately searching for ways of containing the problem, and social workers wishing to rehabilitate the tramp, proposed the establishment of "labor colonies." The State Board of Charities argued in 1908 that the cost of holding 19,843 inmates in the state's jails, workhouses, almshouse and the like was approximately $2,000,000. The labor colony, they contended, would not only reduce costs but would "conduce to the reformation of the tramps and their restoration to self-support and respectability."

The plan was not approved by the legislature until 1911 however. The bill called for the establishment of an "industrial farm colony" for "the detention, humane discipline, instruction, and reformation of male adults committed thereto as tramps or vagrants." While funds were initially allocated and property in upstate New York purchased, an investigative committee one year later recommended that the plans be dropped. The committee cited the expected $1,000,000 construction costs and the anticipated annual maintenance costs as prohibitive factors and stated that it was unwise "for this state to take the initiative in committing itself to such an enormous expense in connection with handling this class of people."[28] Ultimately, the legislature agreed, further funding was withdrawn and the idea of the labor colony faded.

Within the next decade, two more severe economic depressions would confront the nation. Although the almshouse continued to play a central role in poor relief throughout the United States, the character of the institution had begun to change considerably. As can be seen in tables 3.1 and 3.2, not only was the rate of almshouse admissions and those in residence declining but the characteristics of its residents were changing as well. Both trends were reflective of the growth of more specialized facilities which had effectively transferred many residents, with the exception of the elderly. Moreover, the US Bureau of the Census revealed that in 1923, the proportion of those classified as able-bodied resident in almshouses on the census date was just seven percent. The majority (55 percent), were classified as "incapacitated," and the remainder were said to be capable of "light work."[29] Thus, by the mid-1920s, few able-bodied poor were being supported in the public almshouse. How were the majority of the poor cared for by this time? Most survived on a combination of private charity (e.g. bread-lines, soup kitchens, and food, clothing, and coal donations) and increasingly, on public outdoor relief.[30] In New York for example, the State Board of Charities reported that in 1920, county, city, and town poor-law officials expended $1,456,807 on outdoor relief. By 1922, the figure has risen to $2,163,045 while the numbers receiving such relief grew from 56,090 to 87,558 during the period.[31] In Pennsylvania, outdoor relief expenditures by the state's poor boards rose nearly five times during the decade of the 1920s, increasing from 16.4 percent to 42.6 percent of total expenditures. During the same period, expenditures for almshouses across the state rose by only four percent.[32]

Table 3.1 Almshouse trend rates per 100,000 population in residence or admitted during census year: 1880–1923

	Census year				
Type of census count	1880	1890	1904	1910	1923
Resident on census date	132.0	116.6	100.0	91.5	71.5
Admitted during year	NA	NA	99.5	96.0	58.4

Adapted from Paul Lerman, *Deinstitutionalization and the Welfare State* (New Brunswick, NJ: Rutgers University Press, 1982), pp. 34–7. Sources include US Bureau of the Census, *Insane and Feeble-Minded*, 1910; *Feeble-Minded and Epileptics in Institutions*, 1923; *Paupers in Almshouses*, 1923.

Table 3.2 Age distribution of persons residing in almshouses (in percentages)

	Census year				
Age	1880	1890	1904	1910	1923
Under 19	16.2	9.9	4.8	3.8	3.3
20–39	24.0	20.4	13.6	11.2	7.3
40–59	26.7	27.3	28.6	29.4	22.8
60 and over	33.1	40.5	51.2	54.7	65.5
Unknown	–	1.8	1.9	0.8	1.1
Number in sample	(66,203)	(73,044)	(81,764)	(84,198)	(78,090)

Adapted from Lerman, *Deinstitutionalization and the Welfare State*.

This shift away from institutionalization for the able-bodied poor reflected, in part, the overwhelming number of unemployed who were in need of assistance, thereby making institutional relief impossible. Almshouse populations, even at their peak, were at most ten percent of the total unemployed, which, during depressions, were double digit percentages of the civilian population. The state could hardly justify, materially or ideologically, institutionalizing 10 to 20 percent of the population. Moreover, in light of the magnitude of the problem, government officials and the public began to recognize, if only during depressions, that the causes of "mass unemployment" extended beyond individual initiative. State and even federal committees and investigations on unemployment heightened public awareness of the problem, often framing its causes in terms of social and economic problems and frequently making recommendations involving programs for unemployment insurance and future state involvement.[33] Thus, by the late 1920s, more specialized institutions provided for the care and control of the criminal, the delinquent, and the ill. The almshouse, once the symbol of economic dependence and pauperism, was now a home for the infirm and aged rather than an all-purpose institution for a variety of social misfits.

Classification and the Growth of Specialized Institutions

One important development which followed the establishment of state boards of charities in the 1860s was the process of classifying and segregating the population of the almshouse and moving the occupants into facilities designated for their particular "defect." After the creation of the boards, committee investigations recorded the horrid conditions in the "human cesspool" known as the poorhouse, prompting a critical assessment of the house's ability to serve the good of either the public or its inmates. The "crisis" of the mixed almshouse was engendered by a combination of factors. The population of needy dependents, particularly during the depressions, had overwhelmed the institution's ability to even approximate its original goals of "stimulating industry and thrift" or providing "refuge and comfort" to the sick. Rather than "reform" the poor, the institution had become, quite literally, according to its critics, a breeding ground for the next generation of paupers and defectives. Thus from the point of view of both the reformer and the state official, the institution had been a failure at integrating the poor/working class into wage labor, or, for that matter, simply providing humane care for dependents. This failure resulted in such overcrowding and neglect that both the welfare establishment and the public demanded changes.

Reformers contended that the care and control function of the almshouse could be better served if each class of dependent had their own particular needs addressed, since the mixing of such classes had created conditions which were detrimental to all. As Charles Henderson, Professor of Sociology at the University of Chicago stated in his *Introduction to the Study of the Dependent, Defective and Delinquent Classes* in 1893, concerning the conditions of the mixed almshouse:

> Neglect of provisions for entire separation of the sexes leads to immorality, and the same results follow imperfect supervision and classification. The retention of feeble-minded girls and women in poorhouses is a prolific source of illegitimate and defective births, especially if these irresponsible creatures are free to come and go in the intervals of confinement. Feeble-minded women should be held closely in special state asylums their entire lives . . .
>
> The mental sufferings of respectable poor persons which arise from enforced residence with the debased, diseased, criminal, and stupid, are unspeakable, and such compulsory association is a serious wrong to those who have all their lives been industrious and upright . . . One of the worst evils . . . is the residence of children in these abodes of the unfit.[34]

Thus the state attempted to extend administrative rationality and planning (otherwise known as "classification" – the buzzword of reformers) along two related dimensions. The first was the isolation of each particular class of deviants and dependents, not only to physically separate them from each other, but for purposes of more effective surveillance, observation, and control. From a management perspective, specialized facilities would be far easier to administer since they dealt with a single problem population and were more physically secure and isolated from local communities, unlike the chaotic conditions and "revolving door" of the poorhouse. Gender, age, and mental and physical capacities characterized the boundaries between the new facilities which prevented, through the restriction of both social and sexual contact, the procreation of the "defective classes." Secondly, once so isolated, each facility could engage in a more exacting process of distinguishing the degree of each class's "rehabilitative" potential: that is, the extent to which individuals were amenable to entering into labor markets. Whereas custodial care was all that could be expected for the very old, the very young, the infirm, or the completely helpless, others, including recalcitrant children, the healthy deviant, the slightly feeble and the like, could be educated and trained to labor both inside and eventually, outside, the institution.

The first group of dependents affected by the movement for separation were the insane. In New York, the first hospital for the insane in the country was opened in Utica as early as 1843, although the hospital only treated a few hundred "acutely" insane poor who were returned to the almshouse within a year or two if no progress was made. In response to the situation of the chronic insane in poorhouses, the state opened the Willard Asylum in 1869. Willard quickly filled to capacity and expansion became necessary. By 1881, there were six state hospitals for the acute and chronic insane in New York. Throughout other states the trend was similar as asylums proliferated. Between 1850 and 1869, 35 new state hospitals were opened. By 1890, 59 others came into existence, with the post-1870 hospitals being increasingly larger in size.[35] The number of patients in state hospitals rose almost fourfold between 1903 and 1940; from 150,000 to 445,000. As table 3.3 indicates, the rate of commitment to state hospitals more than doubled between 1890 and 1923. This trend continued unabated through the mid 1930s, with the rate reaching 331 per 100,000 by 1935. At the same time, the percentage of mentally ill in the almshouse declined from 24.3 in 1880 to 5.6 in 1923. Moreover, between 1890 and the 1930s, professional psychiatry underwent profound changes. After decades of "therapeutic pessimism," psychiatry was swept into the social and intellectual groundswell of Progressivism – the belief in intelligent and scientific social intervention. A central feature of this emerging mental hygiene movement was the creation of specialized research institutes and laboratory facilities as well as the establishment of

Table 3.3 Trends in institutionalization of almshouse residents, facilities for the insane and feeble-minded: 1890–1923 (per 100,000 population)

Institutions	Census year			
	1890	*1904*	*1910*	*1923*
Almshouse	116.6	100.0	91.5	71.5
Insane asylums	118.2	183.6	204.2	241.7
Facilities for the feeble-minded	8.4	17.5	22.5	39.3
Total	243.2	301.1	318.2	352.5

Adapted from Paul Lerman, *Deinstitutionalization and the Welfare State* (New Brunswick, NJ: Rutgers University Press, 1982), pp. 34–7. Sources include US Bureau of the Census, *Insane and Feeble-Minded*, 1910; *Feeble-Minded and Epileptics in Institutions*, 1923; *Paupers in Almshouses*, 1923.

psychopathic hospitals, psychiatric dispensaries, child guidance clinics and wards of general hospitals.[36] The growth of these professionalized structures and organizational forms not only reflected the expansion of the state's social control sub-apparatus, but aided in the transfer of care for the insane from the almshouse to the asylum.

Children were similarly drawn away from the mixed almshouse where they were, for the most part, "badly fed, badly clothed, badly taken care of, and exposed to the degrading influence of those in immediate charge of them" according to reformer Louisa Lee Schuyler.[37] Nationally, children were removed from the almshouse at a dramatic rate. According to the US Census Bureau, 16.2 percent of almshouse residents were under 19 in 1880; by 1890 the figure was 9.9 and by 1923, this age group represented only 3.3 percent of this population (see table 3.2). In New York, "normal" children over the age of two were prohibited from being committed to the county poorhouse by law in 1875. Of course, this left counties with the problem of disposing of these "deinstitutionalized" children. Many municipalities turned to private, sectarian organizations to care for them. In 1874 there were 132 private orphan asylums and homes for the friendless in New York caring for 11,907 children under 16. By 1885 the numbers were 204 and 23,592. New York City supported 9,363 children in private and public institutions at a cost of $757,858 in the year the law was enacted, 1875. A decade later, the City transferred $1,526, 517 to private facilities alone to care for nearly 15,000 young people.[38]

In addition to the use of private facilities to care for the dependent child, other states took alternative routes: public institutions were opened in 20 states on the "Michigan" plan; three others on the county children's homes of Ohio; and "boarding-out" systems were publicly administered in Massachusetts and New Jersey and by private agencies in Pennsylvania.[39] Moreover, specialized juvenile correction facilities – "houses of refuge," "reformatories," and "training schools" – expanded both the classification scheme and the system of care and control of dependent and troublesome children. Not only were children increasingly institutionalized in segregated facilities, but the legal mechanisms by which they got there changed as well. In one more manifestation of the Bureaucratic State and the trend toward administrative reform and rationality, within 25 years of the adoption of the first juvenile court legislation in Illinois in 1899, courts were established in every state but two. While perhaps more ceremonial than substantive at first, the juvenile court evolved to possess broad-sweeping jurisdiction over the lives of children under the age of 16.[40] The courts' ideological foundation rested on the notion of *parens patriae*, and thus the legal institution was charged with protecting and providing for the needs of delinquent, dependent and neglected youth.

Specialized facilities were also developed for the "feebleminded" and the epileptic. "Mental defectives" were further classified as "teachable" or "unteachable." New York had established a state school for the feeble-minded in Syracuse in 1855; but it was soon crowded with those incapable of learning. The state responded to the unteachable feeble-minded in 1894 with the Rome State Custodial Asylum – the first of its kind in the US. The state also founded the Craig Colony for epileptics in 1896. Nationally, table 3.3 indicates that the rate of institutionalization at feeble-minded and epileptic facilities rose from 8.4 per 100,000 in 1890 to 39.3 by 1923. Despite these specialized institutions, these classes were not removed as expediently from the almshouse as others. Of those characterized as defective in 1923, the feeble-minded accounted for 33 percent of the almshouse residents on the census date, outnumbered only by the crippled.

Concerned with the "hereditary factor" in the proliferation of crime, pauperism, and mental deficiency, reformers and state welfare administrators sought to isolate its source – "the unrestrained liberty allowed to vagrant and degraded women;" this the conclusion of a report by Mrs Josephine Lowell in 1878, a member of the State Board of Charities of New York. Three years earlier, Mrs Lowell was instrumental in creating the State Custodial Asylum for Feeble-minded Women at Newark. She had argued that there was need for a custodial asylum for feeble-minded women of childbearing age. This, in the words of David Schneider and Albert Deutsch, would "protect them from the evils of society to which they were especially susceptible and would spare society the expense of supporting their tainted progeny."[41] Using the same reasoning and armed with the Hoyt report of 1876 which chronicled the deviant exploits of poorhouse women, Mrs Lowell urged the creation of an institution for "vagrant and degraded" women which, if not achieving reformation, could at least cut off the line of pauper descendance. The campaign resulted in the House of Refuge for Women at Hudson in 1887 where "all females between the ages of 15 and 30 years who have been convicted of petty larceny, habitual drunkenness, of being common prostitutes, frequenters of disorderly houses or houses of prostitution" were to be placed. Suitable employment was to be provided which would encourage "habits of self supporting industry" and "mental and moral improvement." It was soon filled to capacity and three other women's reformatories were erected in the state by the late 1890s. Again, this specialization was reflected in the chang-

ing demographics of the almshouse nationwide as the ratio of
men to 100 women, slightly favoring men in 1880 at 116.1, rose
to 223.7 men to 100 women by 1923.[42]

Absorbing the Local State: Centralization, Political Power, and the State Apparatus

The United States changed dramatically during the years from
the mid-nineteenth century to the 1920s. Through waves of
immigration, the population of the country had more than
doubled during the period – the majority now clustered in
urban areas. Gross national product, in constant dollars, was
nearly four times the 1885 figure by 1929. Accompanying these
changes was an increasing complexity to social life and the
problems it generated. For throughout this period, cyclical and
severe economic depressions had produced double digit unemployment, record capitalist bankruptcies, and considerable
working-class unrest. Such social and economic crises laid the
basis for increased state intervention in an attempt to cope with
the destructive aspects of a fluctuating business cycle; the social
"costs" of private accumulation.

With the rise of an urban and monopolized industrial formation we see a corresponding change in the form of the state, the
functions it prioritized, and the apparatus through which it
exercised its power. This process is clearly evident within the
evolving social control sub-apparatus. Here as I have demonstrated, lower-tiered political entities such as local municipalities
were increasingly overshadowed by the upper-levels of the state
hierarchy; first by townships, then the counties, and finally by
state level agencies. This eclipse of the local state took numerous forms: the passing of legislation which mandated certain
practices; the provision of financial inducements to conform to
policy shifts; and the removal of jurisdiction over certain
populations and the creation of a higher-tiered institutions and
apparatus. This movement was not simply a shift in bureaucra-

tic arrangement or organization. Rather it reflected a consolidation of political power, which in turn, resulted in an expansion of the state apparatus, and ultimately, in increased state control over social life. What were the forces and logic behind this reconstitution of state power and the rise of the "Bureaucratic State?"

The first was related to the state's role in crisis management and the unintended consequences of earlier policies. The growing intensity of social problems and the apparent failure of the state to deal with these difficulties triggered a search for alternative strategies. For example, following the Panic of 1819 and the recommendations of the Yates Report concerning the inadequacy of local relief efforts, New York State erected county poorhouses. Within two decades the fiscal and administrative failure of the "mixed" almshouse to cope with economic displacement prompted the establishment of a central State Board. The result of this action was the accelerated growth of specialized State controlled facilities and eventually, the virtual abandonment of the local, all-purpose almshouse. What was the logic behind the centralization of authority? In the first place, before any informed decisions could be made, an authorized agency, having the power to inspect and enforce compliance, was necessary to collect information. The nineteenth-century legislative committees of "experts" investigating the poor laws compiled some of America's first social statistics. They laid the organization and professional groundwork and the justification of centralized administration. Secondly, as the argument goes, consolidating the supervision of relief would result in increased coordination, efficiency in management, and even financial savings. As the authors of a Massachusetts legislative committee argued in prefacing a call for the first "state board" in 1858:

> Each of these new [state controlled lunatic hospitals, reformatories and almshouses] institutions has been created without any special reference to others, and in no degree as part of a uniform system. It happens accordingly that there are anomalies in the organization and management, increasing the expense of conducting them and

> impairing their efficiency ... for instance, the lunatic
> hospitals have five trustees each, the reform and industrial
> schools, seven each, and the almshouses and pauper hos-
> pital three each ... a want of symmetry so palpable on the
> surface betrays an absence of a system – of adaptation of
> different parts to each other – which cannot fail to produce
> confusion and loss.[43]

Similarly, reformers and State Board members used this argument to justify the creation and expansion of specialized
institutions in an attempt to extend administrative rationality
and planning.

And yet, these notions aside, the centralization of authority
and the eventual expansion of the social control apparatus was
as much about reproducing the state itself as it was about
solving problems of deviancy and dependency. Let us return to
the case of Massachusetts. While local responsibility formed the
basic principle of poor relief, the province had made concilia-
tory provisions to local communities for some unsettled poor:
as early as 1675 for reimbursing the towns for the refugees of
King Philip's War; in 1700 for those traveling from abroad who
became ill during the voyage; in 1767 for the cost of conveyance
of those with settlement outside the province; and finally, in
1794, the Commonwealth took responsibility for the unsettled
husband of a settled wife.[44] Eager to defray costs, communities
took advantage of this last "loophole" and labelled as many as
they could "state paupers." To send the pauper away involved
expense. By providing sub-standard care, towns could actually
gain revenues under the plan. Reimbursement to towns for the
unsettled poor rose from $14,000 in 1792–3 to $27,000 by 1798.
Between 1826 and 1831 the State Treasurer paid out
$284,584.29 to cities and towns for the unsettled poor.[45]

The Quincy Report in 1821 called for the establishment of a
system of district almshouses "having reference to placing the
whole subject of the poor of the Commonwealth under the
regular and annual superintendence of the Legislature."[46]
Efforts were made to tighten requirements but the affects were
minimal, particularly in the face of what one citizen called the

"host of intemperate and quarrelsome stragglers" from abroad who were supported by the state. Yet, reluctant to discourage immigration of the industrious alien, the state created the Board of Alien Commissioners in 1851 which was authorized to enforce all legislation concerning immigration (principally to invoke laws restricting the alien poor and sick from emigrating) and support of the state poor. This body recommended and saw through the creation of three state almshouses/farms, where the state pauper would finally be put to work, and a hospital for paupers and dependents. The creation of these state facilities – in addition to three state mental hospital, two reform schools and four charitable institutions which received state support – led to the call for a centralized overseer: the State Board of Charities.

Here we see how a whole set of institutions was erected not for the principal reason of providing for the indigent, but rather for one level of the state hierarchy to gain control over expenditures and to consolidate its power, both of which were being exploited at the local level. The result however was only a small reduction in the number of "state paupers" supported locally, and the creation of a new sub-apparatus of the state which were soon filled to capacity. Moreover, the history of the state Board, created to coordinate the system, reveals the dilemma of centralization – the entrenchment of personal and professional interests where issues of organizational status and reproduction dominate. With the exception of one Board member designated an "agent of the state," the members were unpaid appointees of the governor. They held offices in the state house, could hire assistance, and controlled an annual appropriation. Composed of medical doctors, philanthropists, and reformers, the Board was intended to operate outside the sphere of political influence; a "lay" supervisory group if you will.

As social reformers, Board members were in a position to evoke scandal and criticize state policy; "The reformers used words, charts and pictures as their weapons. They aimed for the sympathy of the wider public, or, more tellingly, at a public sense of social costs."[47] The State Board of Charities moved quickly to consolidate its power. In its second report the Board recommended a reclassification of the state almshouses, reasserting the idea that they be workhouses for the able-bodied, and calling for the segregation of the insane and the idiotic and children and thereby extending their organizational reach. By its third year it held the authority to enact these ideas as well as to require private charities to submit annual reports and, eventually, require licensing. The Board would further permeate these "private" organizations by providing state grants only under the condition that Board appointed trustees be part of the directorates.[48] Yet with their growing power and authority, the Board moved from being "outside" the state, to being representatives *of* the state and its policies. In 1870 for example, the Board of Charities was compelled to reply to charges that the state mental hospitals were mistreating patients. As Grob noted: "Both the Board and the individual state institutions . . . were confronted with rising public suspicion and distrust of their work." It was publicly charged that the lunatic hospitals were being used as "bastiles for the imprisonment of insane persons, for wicked purposes."[49] The Board was now in a position of having to defend the *status quo* rather than to challenge it.

But the Board's power was not absolute; it was embedded in a complex web of interest and authority. Despite its far-reaching authority, the state Board did not have a say over the day-to-day operations of the institutions themselves. Thus they often had to negotiate and compromise with other powerful state agents in other sectors of the state apparatus. For example, in 1870 the Superintendent of Worcester Lunatic Hospital, Merrick Bemis, advanced a plan to build a new state hospital organized on the decentralized "cottage plan" of the colony at Gheel, Belgium. Despite the somewhat radical nature of the proposal, it received support from the hospital trustees, the Board of Charities, the legislature, and even the Governor who signed the plan into law. Yet it was Bemis' own colleagues who began to speak out against the new facility. Some spoke of the expected higher costs of the arrangement, while others saw the less restrictive environment proposed as a threat to surrounding communities. In reality, hospital superintendents in Massachusetts (and others around the country) saw the "cottage plan" as a threat to their own power which the centralized hospital reproduced and which was the institutional basis of their burgeoning professional psychiatric authority.

First to speak out against the plan was Pliny Earle, Superintendent of Northampton hospital and nationally recognized psychiatric figure. Others followed. The state Board, quick to sense the changing sentiments and undoubtedly not wanting to confront the independent and professional power of the superintendents, quickly retreated from their support of the plan, even denying their original support. In the end, Merrick Bemis resigned under a cloud of controversy and the State of Massachusetts got itself a new centralized custodial asylum on the grounds at Worcester. In 1879, the Board of Charities itself was subsumed – along with the Board of Health and nine other Boards overseeing state institutions – into the State Board of Health, Lunacy and Charity. Power converged, the apparatus grew, and the Bureaucratic State triumphed.

PART II

Accumulating Minds and Bodies

Social Control and the American State, 1930–1985

4

Charting the Advanced-Capitalist State

The depression of the 1930s began a 20-year period of adjustment and transformation for American society. The conditions that ushered in this era were both severe and dramatic. The country's rise as an industrial power was built upon fundamental changes in the nature of American capitalism, bringing about a realignment of class relations in the context of urbanization as well as changes in technology, communications, and organization. What is clear is that the social and economic formation of American society was changing and so was the nature of the American state. The rise of what I have called the "Bureaucratic State" was the initial response to these changes, reflected in the centralization and genuine bureaucratization of state governments and the rise of national administrative capacities.

Yet the power of this new governmental order was clearly tested, first with the depression of the thirties and then with world war. These crises provided the catalyst for the emergence of a postwar capital-labor accord, the rise of powerful transnational corporations, permanent state fiscal management, and the development and expansion of policies and practices associated with contemporary welfare states. I want to characterize this emerging social formation as "advanced-capitalist" and delineate two advanced-capitalist state forms. The first was a transition "Crisis State" (roughly 1930 to the early 1950s). Actions by this state provided both the ideological justification and the material means for the structuration of the existing social control sub-apparatus. While hesitant and relatively conservative in its response, the Crisis State and the events of the depression and world war ultimately laid a partial foundation for the emergence of the American "Liberal Welfare State" (roughly 1950 to the present). It is under this state that we see the development of explicit state policies to coordinate economic production and consumption, aided by both organized labor and capital. Social welfare legislation during the period developed incrementally, as the result of compromises between political parties and bureaucratic interests now lodged firmly in the expanding apparatus of the federal government. Moreover, as I will demonstrate, the interests of powerful professional and economic groups constituted within the welfare/health/penal sub-apparatus created potential conflicts in public policies goals and directions.

The Crisis State

The decade of the 1930s saw one of the worst economic declines in modern history. During the first three years of that period, the gross national product of the United States, in constant dollars, fell just over 30 percent. The national index of factory employment plummeted from 110.3 in 1929 to an average of 92.4 in 1930, 78.1 in 1931, 66.3 in 1932 and to a low of 62.3 in March of 1933. By that year, banks had failed on the average of 241 a month; nearly five times the rate prior to the fall of 1929. And, according to official estimates, nearly one in four Americans was unemployed; 24.9 percent or 12,830,000 members of the civilian labor force were out of work.[1] Labor organizations and others contended that the numbers were much higher. As the depression spread throughout the West, reactions ranged from the outbreak of authoritarian fascism to liberal reformist political coalitions.[2] In the United States, although capitalism was never really contested by any political formations, the events of the period did give rise to significant changes in economic theory, the political process, and the role of the state in social life.[3] According to Stephen Skowronek, the expansion of institutional capacities during Roosevelt's second term completed the state building process set in motion during the Progressive period. He argues:

> The major constructive contribution of the New Deal to the operation of the new American state lay in the sheer expansion of bureaucratic services and supports. Pushing courts and party organizations further out of the center of government operations, the New Deal turned bureaucracy itself into the extraconstitutional machine so necessary for the continuous operation of the constitutional system. Like party patronage in the old order, bureaucratic goods and services came to provide the fuel and the cement of the new institutional politics.[4]

Beginning with the Wagner Act and proceeding through Social Security legislation and the Reorganization Act of 1937, these "emergency" measures were soon a permanent part of the executive sub-apparatus of the state. Moreover, these reforms institutionalized "the *power* of the New Dealers by establishing a set of institutions which would link the administration to a mass constituency, and would enable it to assert control over the entire governmental structure . . ."[5] These changes therefore embedded the interests of a new class of state managers in the executive apparatus. As Edward Berkowitz and Kim McQuiad have argued, despite some legislative failures, "a remarkable growth in the number of federal personnel concerned with social welfare, a definite change in the government's bureaucratic structure, and a marked growth in confidence among those who administered social welfare programs occurred between 1934 and 1943."[6]

What effect did the crisis of the depression and this "state building" process have on institutional social control? In the short run, their combination served to bolster the existing social control sub-apparatus. On the one hand, the depression (and later the war) deflected public attention away from the conditions and consequences of America's rapidly growing institutionalized populations. On the other hand, the relief and public

works policies of the federal government, aimed at alleviating
the distress of the depression, ensured not only the continuation
of bureaucratic goods and services, but real expansion of the
institutional apparatus. State and city governments, already
burdened by over-expansion and debt incurred during the
1920s, were overwhelmed with the onset of the depression.
These levels of government took full advantage of incoming
federal grants and public works dollars to replenish budgets and
to rebuild and expand the public infrastructure (e.g. roads,
schools, hospitals, and the like). Thus during the period of the
Crisis State, we see a well-entrenched, state-level, sub-
apparatus further legitimized and supported by changes in the
larger political economy. Moreover, as I will demonstrate, the
contradictions and consequences embedded in these state organizations hindered their ability to accomplish their intended
purpose. Indeed, rather than transforming their changes,
through therapy and correction, into productive citizens, these
facilities became warehouses for the accumulation of minds and
bodies.

The Liberal Welfare State

While the depression of the 1930s set the stage for the establishment of state fiscal management, it was not until the war that
the US economy actually recovered and, moreover, not until
the post-war period that the government engaged in anything
like Keynesian-style macroeconomic policy. Many believed
that the large budgets and deficits initiated during the mid 1920s
and continued through the early 1940s represented an
"emergency" response to economic collapse and international
war. Yet by war's end, influential economists began to argue
that private business investment was no longer able to sustain
the kind of steady growth needed to avoid a recurrence of the
1930s, and that government spending and monetary regulation
were necessary to supplement growth and to counter destructive cycles.[7] But if state coordinated economic production and
consumption were to be obtained, a degree of consensus would

have to be achieved among what was left of the New Deal political coalition.[8] Evidence suggests that the Truman administration was able to forge a "postwar settlement" in the late 1940s composed of New Deal social welfare advocates, Cold War protagonists, and representatives of both organized labor (purged of its left-wing influences) and corporate capital. The strategy this coalition settled on in order to obtain the goals of economic growth, to counter periodic crises, to provide employment, and to insure social integration through minimum welfare guarantees was government spending – principally military expenditures.[9] This made it possible, as Martin Shefter notes, "to give all the major actors in American politics a stake in the nation's national security policies, and therefore in its postwar regime."[10] I want to characterize this postwar regime as a "Liberal Welfare State," constituted by its level of intervention in the economic and social/cultural spheres relative to other contemporary "welfare" states.[11]

The combination of the postwar "accord" and the dominance of American capital in the world market created a period of vigorous economic expansion. Yet with few exceptions, prosperity created conditions which undermined rather than supported the development of national social welfare measures put in place during the depression and the war. Private "fringe benefits" tied to the work place rather than public sector welfare programs would be the soul of America's "welfare state."[12] Thus those state managers in the federal bureaucracy with interests in expanding social welfare programs confronted an unreceptive executive branch. While Truman was willing to defend existing public welfare programs, according to Berkowitz and McQuiad, his administration was concerned with the explosive growth of the federal bureaucracy through the crisis of depression and war.[13] This conservatism was followed by Eisenhower as well: "The Republicans entered office . . . with an optimistic faith in their ability to tame a previous untractable public sector through prudent management."[14] During this period there was an attempt to shift responsibility for social welfare functions back to the states, recreating those fiscal and political troubles of the 1920s at the local level which had been temporarily alleviated by the federal "emergency" response. We see therefore, in the mid-1950s, the first evidence of a reversal in the nearly 200-year-old trend of increasing institutionalization, as state governments confronted the problems of a highly centralized, aging and costly social control apparatus.

From the postwar until the early 1960s, social welfare in the US developed in incremental fashion, reflecting the struggles between political parties, bureaucratic interest, and major private actors (both professional and economic). Not until the mid 1960s did bureaucratic goods and services from the federal government expand as they had during the New Deal, and become part and parcel of a new attempt at state building. The emerging ideological critique of the "total institution" was articulated into policy at the federal level by the Kennedy administration, since the rhetoric of this movement centering on "the community" meshed well with this regime's progressive social reforms, its political strategy, and its macroeconomic goals. In the post-1965 period we saw a massive public "deinstitutionalization," "decriminalization," and "diversion" movement in which the care and correction of troublesome individuals would become decentralized and take place "in the community." But as I will demonstrate in coming chapters, the political and economic contradictions embedded in this strategy blew apart the postwar accord, setting the stage for the spiraling inflation and "fiscal crisis" of the 1970s and the politically conservative 1980s.

Crucial to this historical development, and central to understanding contemporary trends in social control, has been the extent to which the interests of professional and socioeconomic groups *outside* the state have been constituted *within* the welfare/health/penal sub-apparatus. Overshadowed by the integration of large corporate entities in the development of the "military-industrial complex," there has also been a similar trend in the what is now being called the "medical-industrial complex." Here professional, corporate and individual interests have become powerful forces in shaping public policy and taking advantage of swelling welfare state expenditures. For example, the American Medical Association and other medical groups joined forces with federal officials in the Public Health Services to push for such legislation as the National Mental Health Act and the Hospital Survey and Construction Act of 1946. These bills increased federal expenditures for US health care while assuring that private groups controlled how the monies were spent. As I will demonstrate, the proliferation of these kinds of developments before and during the public decarceration movement of the 1960s helped shape the emergence of a new state apparatus characterized by decentralization and "privatization." But first, let us begin by considering the evolution of the social control sub-apparatus under conditions of the Crisis State.

Roads to the State Asylum

Despite several decades of Progressive challenges to the asylum, during the first half of the nineteenth century, the state hospital was more entrenched than ever. In fact, as I shall argue, the evidence suggests that attempts by reformers and professionals to alter the role of the institution during the early years of the twentieth century may have had the opposite effect of bolstering its bureaucratic structure and organizational legitimacy. That is, so called "alternatives" to the asylum actually became organizational appendages to the institution. Between 1935 and 1955, the population in state and county facilities increased from 388,534 to 558,922 while federal (Veterans) hospitals rose from 23,000 to 60,000. Overall, these populations increased at a rate per 100,000 population from 331 in 1935 to 390 in 1955.[15] By that later date, while there were 275 state and county hospitals out of a total of 1,699 mental health facilities, state hospitals accounted for nearly half of patient care episodes. The annual number of state hospital admissions during the period rose from just over 100,000 in 1935 to 185,597 in 1955.[16] What accounts for the dramatic rise in state hospital populations during the first half of the twentieth century? Demographically at least, the increasing population of the state hospitals reflected an age-specific movement. In 1910, the number of residents in state hospitals 65 years or older per 100,000 in the population was 554; by 1923 it was 700 and by 1950 it was 1,150.[17] This trend was the result of the shifting of care for the elderly from the local level, i.e. the almshouse, to the state level. As the previous chapter demonstrated, with the rise in state responsibility and specialized facilities near the end of the nineteenth century, most classes of almshouse residents were transferred to these newer state-run institutions, except for the elderly. Yet the elderly, too, would soon be moved out of the almshouse. Gerald Grob summarized the dynamics of the trend as

> less a function of medical or humanitarian concerns than a consequence of financial considerations. As states began to adopt and implement the principles of state responsibility for all insane persons . . . local public officials seized upon the fiscal advantages inherent in redefining senility in psychiatric terms. If senile persons could be cared for in state hospitals rather than in local or county almshouses, the burden of support could be transferred to the state.[18]

While there were an increasing number of elderly at risk in the general population, the rates per 100,000 indicate that the state hospital had become *the* care and control setting for the destitute and the physically or mentally impaired elderly.

With state governments assuming increasing fiscal responsibilities between the 1890s and the 1920s, this level of government was soon overwhelmed during the depression of the 1930s since it was already engaged in deficit spending. A large part of the federal response to the economic crisis involved a massive infusion of dollars into public works programs and direct aid to states. According to the Public Works Administration (PWA) records, half of the PWA apportionment for hospitals was used in the construction of facilities for the mentally ill. With funds exceeding $14 million, the Administration added nearly 50,000 beds for the mentally ill during the late 1930s.[19] Because spending for the hospitals was already a fixed part of state budgets and because of federal backing during the depression and beyond, the financial status of the state mental hospital was never threatened, even during the depression. In his study, Grob characterizes the situation this way:

> Generally speaking, state mental hospitals suffered less than other public institutions. Between 1929 and 1930 per capita expenditures at all state hospitals fell from $312 to $302, but dollar purchasing power may have risen because of a declining price level . . . By 1940 per capita expenditures had nearly reached pre-depression levels. A study conducted by the NCMH [National Committee for Mental Hygiene] concluded that budget reductions had little impact upon institutionalized patients.[20]

In the late 1940s, appropriations for the state hospitals continued to rise. Maintenance expenditures alone, in constant dollars, had nearly tripled by 1955.[21] This is not to say that the hospitals were adequately funded or that additional bed space kept up with demand. In fact, throughout most of the first half of the twentieth century, the average facility was overcrowded, under-staffed, and under-budgeted for the task at hand.[22] Rather, one factor in creating the "enduring asylum" was that the institution was caught up in the dynamics of the political economy of the period. In the first stage (pre-depression), local communities seized the opportunity to shift care to state governments which were assuming a greater role in institutional social control given the "crisis" of the mixed almshouse and the centralization of state governments. The state hospital was seen, at the time, as a cost effective alternative to local care. In the second stage (post-depression), the federal response to the economic down-turn was a massive infusion of dollars and labor into public works, which, given the lack of alternatives or any incentive to find one, propped up the state hospital and ensured its fiscal survival.

Medical and professional factors also played a role in the spiral of patient numbers at state hospitals. Even fairly crude diagnostic data indicate the chronic nature of the cases sent to the hospitals and the dismal prospects for their cure and release. Over half of the admissions to state facilities in 1922 were, by most standards, classified as incurable; the senile (16 percent) the syphilitic (11 percent), the alcoholic (4 percent), the retarded (3 percent), and the schizophrenic (23 percent).[23] Little had changed by 1939 except that a larger percentage of schizophrenics (45 percent) were present and, as David Rothman concluded in surveying the situation, "fully 54 percent [of the patients] had remained in the institution for five years or more – and a little over one-third of the patients were residents over ten years. A commitment to a state hospital meant a stay of a very long time."[24] In Grob's study of Massachusetts, he reports that

> Between 1929 and 1937 the average length of hospital confinement rose from 8.9 to 9.7 years. Put in a slightly different way, out of every 1,000 first admissions in 1937, 167 were returned to the community and 86 died; for readmitted persons the respective figures were 113 and 35. The most astonishing statistic was the total number of patients retained in hospitals; 746 out of every 1,000 first admissions and 851 out of every [1,000] readmissions remained institutionalized at the end of the year.[25]

Moreover, while admission to the hospital left the average patient with little chance of early release and with the potential for abuse and maltreatment, the minimal amount of care provided and the safety of the institutional environment probably had increased the longevity of hospital patients.

Professional factors and reformist movements set in motion during the turn of the century also contributed to the increased use of the state hospital, often in direct opposition to stated intentions. Urged by the criticisms of both other professionals and lay reformers and the recent "advances" in treatment by their European counterparts, American psychiatrists began a reflective assessment of their practice, focusing on the inadequacy of the very institution from which their profession had arisen: the asylum. As Dr Landon Gray stated to the American Neurological Association in 1896, "We are startled to find that no type of mental disease, no original pathological observation, no new departure in treatment, and not one text-book, has ever come from an American asylum despite the millions of dollars and thousands of patients they have had at their command."[26]

Armed with a new sense of optimism concerning the potential treatment of mental illness, individuals such as Adolf Myers and Clifford Beers set out to establish a more scientific investigation of insanity. As we have seen, the organizational forms instituted during the mental hygiene movement were research institutes and laboratory facilities as well as psychopathic hospitals, psychiatric dispensaries, child guidance clinics and general hospital wards. The research institutes, set up in both state hospitals and at medical schools and teaching universities, were intended to bring scientific research into the asylums as well as to establish institutional linkages to the country's medical training and research facilities. Advances in scientific psychiatry, it was thought, would change the custodial character of the state facilities (now symbolically renamed "hospitals" rather than "asylums"), and reduce our dependence on them. The goal of the psychopathic hospital and clinic was the screening, observation, and "cure and prevention" of acute mental disease, providing outpatient services, encouraging home care, and to provide a clinical setting for students of psychiatry. Yet, encumbered by controversies between the hospital staff and the institute directors over organizational objectives, bureaucratic authority, and the very bases of psychiatric practice, the success of the research institute in advancing both the scientific study of mental illness and the lives of state hospital patients was limited. Over time, most retreated, in spirit and in practice, to university settings.[27]

The experience of the psychopathic hospital was equally unimpressive in achieving its stated goals. In fact, rather than "diagnostic centers" which reduced reliance on the asylum, the psychopathic facility became, paradoxically, an organizational appendage to the state hospital itself. The lack of both real therapeutic technologies and legal obstacles to temporary commitments, as well as the convenience to families and physicians in initiating this first step to commitment through these facilities, created an accumulation of incurable and increased referrals to the state hospital. As an example, 40 to 50 percent of the patients admitted to the Syracuse Psychopathic ended up in state hospitals.[28]

In sum, and in more current social control terminology, the psychopathic hospital, in its various forms, had "widened the net" of the mental health system by expanding its bureaucratic structure and reach. While these developments were set in motion during the previous period, the accumulated effects of this contradiction were carried over. Moreover, rather than bringing science into the mental hospital, the professionalization of modern psychiatry actually distanced its practice from the institution. By associating itself with medical and research training facilities, psychiatry had gained professional legitimacy. Yet, given the custodial nature of the mental hospital and the expanding occupational opportunities for psychiatrists, the profession had little incentive to associate itself with what some considered to be an archaic institution. "The role of caretaker for individuals who were socially marginal and who lacked either resources or families (or both) was frowned upon by a speciality that defined its mission in medical and scientific terms."[29]

Finally, other evidence suggests that the state hospitals became, in part, a social control repository for the odd, the nonconformist, the misbehaved, and the misunderstood, thereby contributing to their explosive population growth. In his study of the California system during the turn of the century, Richard Fox contends, in reference to the psychopathic hospital, that professionals and reformers failed to see or acknowledge how local community authorities were wedded to the more traditional reliance on the asylum for their social control needs.[30] Their goal, the author states, was "the confinement of individuals who, whether mentally ill or not, seemed to threaten family stability or public tranquility."[31] And while the time frame of Fox's study is early in the century, there is little to suggest that this social control function of the state hospital diminished significantly between the 1930s and the 1950s.

Fox chronicles, through case histories, the stories of lives caught up on the road to the state hospital. One example:

In the summer of 1906 the San Francisco police arrested a 52-year-old Canadian-born vagrant for "wandering the streets." Judging the man's behavior "irrational," they took him to the Detention Hospital. After one night in his cell the medical examiner checked him, noting that he was "quiet, [and] refuses to answer questions." Despite his silence, however, he was clearly, in the medical examiner's opinion, "unable to care for himself." The doctor recommended commitment and the following day – 48 hours after the police had picked him up – a sheriff's deputy escorted him to the Napa State Hospital, were he would remain confined for at least three months, and perhaps a good deal longer.[32]

Other persons who were eventually committed to one of the state hospitals between 1900 and 1930 included a woman with no occupation who "repeatedly" wore "a sailor's uniform," used "foul language," and who was declared a "public nuisance;" a self-referred Englishman who sought treatment for an opium addiction; a 25-year-old prostitute who "persistently refused" treatment for syphilis and was declared a "menace to society;" and finally, there was the 40-year-old Russian-born housewife who was detained after her husband accused her of making "foolish purchases." She was placed on parole, but after further difficulties, was committed to Napa State hospital. Again, the application of such a broadly-defined notion of "mentally ill' was not confined to the early years of the twentieth century. Other evidence suggests that it may have persisted for decades to come, contributing to the swelling populations of the state hospital. For example, Carol Warren examines the relationship between the family and the mental hospitalization of women in the 1950s, revealing the notion of role performance as an indicator of mental illness and the relative ease in which men were able to commit their wives.[33]

Thus a number of factors contributed to the unyielding dominance of the state hospital as *the* setting for the treatment of mental illness during the first half of the twentieth century. Yet change was on the horizon. The end of World War II marked the beginning of significant federal participation in public mental health concerns. In partial response to the apparently staggering rates of mental illness among inductees and those prematurely discharged from the armed forces, the federal government initiated plans to address this public health problem. Most notable was the passage of the National Mental Health Act of 1946 (PL-487), the purpose of which was

> the improvement of the mental health of the people of the United States through the conducting of researches, investigations, experiments, and demonstrations relating to the cause, diagnosis, and treatment of psychiatric disorders; assisting and fostering such research activities by public and private agencies, and promoting the coordination of such researches and activities and the useful application of these results; training personnel in matters relating to mental health; and developing and assisting States in the use of, the most effective methods of prevention, diagnosis, and treatment of psychiatric disorders.

To accomplish this goal, the Act established a National Advisory Council, sponsored national health conferences, provided grants to states of up to $30,000,000 per year, as well as the sum of $7,500,000 for the creation of the National Institute of Mental Health – the coordinating organization for the Act's provisions.

Claiming successful treatments of war-related mental illness, military psychiatrists returned eager to apply new treatment modes in civilian settings, including narcosynthesis, hypnosis, short-term therapy, and group therapy.[34] Psychiatric wards were established in the already established Veterans Administration system of hospitals under the guidance of Daniel Blain, head of psychiatric services. Once again, a renewed sense of optimism concerning the treatment of mental illness had emerged. "Modern science," claimed Kenneth Appel in his presidential address to the APA (American Psychiatric Association) in 1954, "offers new challenges, possibilities, and optimism" for confronting the neglect of the mentally ill.[35]

Finally, federal participation in setting a national mental health policy agenda in this period came with the passage of the "Mental Health Study Act of 1955" (PL-182). This Act created the Joint Commission of Mental Illness and Health, an interdisciplinary body formed with members of the American Psychiatric Association and the American Medical Association and charged with assessing the mental health needs of the nation. Although the Joint Commission's reports would not appear for more than five years after the Commission's formation, these documents would provide an ideological manifesto for the advocates of community-based mental health treatment and spell an end to the dominance of the state asylum on the institutional landscape of America.

The Idle and Unproductive in the Penitentiary

In the 1930s, the situation in adult prisons was considered quite bleak even among the most optimistic of correctional reformers.[36] Inmate populations had increased dramatically; between 1926 and 1939 the population in federal and state facilities had risen to a pre-war peak from 96,125 to 179,818.[37] Not coincidental to this rise, in 1929, a number of riots had occurred in addition to a fire in the Ohio state prison at Columbus which killed 322. Moreover, investigative studies began to uncover alarming rates of recidivism and the ineffectiveness of rehabilitation efforts. Prison industries had come to a virtual standstill given the restrictive legislation passed during the previous decade, the dominance of state-use account systems, and the economic depression.[38] The extent of prison idleness prompted Sanford Bates, Director of the Federal Bureau of Prisons, to state in 1933 that

broadly speaking, the prisons of the country seem no nearer a solution of the employment problem than they were in 1923. I think I cannot be contradicted when I say that today there is more idleness in most of the prisons of the country than ever. Those private manufacturers affected are more vociferous and uncompromising in their attitude than heretofore; labor is still unsatisfied; and the public remains uninformed and indifferent.[39]

Various attempts were made by public and prison officials to loosen the constraints of the Hawes–Cooper Act of 1929 which had severely restricted the interstate flow of prison goods. Not unlike other interest groups during this time, these parties sought the assistance of the federal government concerning prison industries. Soon after the passage of the National Industrial Recovery Act in 1933, the National Recovery Administration (NRA) received proposals by both industrial trade associations *and* prison administrators who were attempting to influence the codes for competition and trade concerning prison goods. After a number of meetings it became clear to those correctional officials advocating the less restrictive approach outlined in their Prison Industries Code submitted to the NRA, that the provisions of the Recovery Act itself would not permit adoption of their measures. That is, all codes considered under the NRA were required to contain a provision for collective bargaining (section 7a – included to ensure the support of organized labor) which of course the states would not recognize given that the workers were prisoners.

Undaunted, prison and state officials set about arranging a voluntary pact concerning the sale and distribution of prison-made goods. By spring of 1934, 28 governors or prison authorities had signed the agreement, which was later approved by the President.[40] Following the signing of the pact, the President appointed a three-member board, representing labor, industry, and consumers, forming the Prison Labor Authority which was to hear complaints and protests. Later in 1934, pressure applied to the NRA by industry organizations resulted in the appointment of the Ulman Committee to investigate the operation of the Prison Labor Compact and the Prison Labor Authority. Testimony from both industry and labor soundly criticized current practices. The Ulman Committee's final report advocated the establishment of a 50-million-dollar fund within the Public Works Administration for the reorganization of prison industries which would include a completely closed (non-market participation), state-use system to avoid any competition with free manufacturers and labor.

Following the disintegration of the NRA, Roosevelt established the Prison Industries Reorganization Administration (PRIA) in September 1935. Supported by funds from the Emergency Relief Appropriations Act, the PRIA surveyed 22 state prison systems and made recommendations concerning the organization of their industries and penal systems. In coordination with state authorities, the PRIA had a limited degree of success in aiding states in the reorganization of state-use accounts, education and recreational programs, classification schemes, and the establishment or modification of parole and probation systems. Moreover, in coordination with the Public Works Administration, PRIA plans included the construction of new prisons and a variety of "medium" and "minimum" secure facilities such as camps, farms, and the like.

Within the Federal prison system, James Bennett, a leading member of the Federal Prison Bureau, had managed, with much political maneuvering, to secure a bill in 1937 creating the Federal Prison Industries, Inc. – a non-profit management corporation. According to Blake McKelvey, "Under its vigorous management a group of diversified industries was developed which not only met production costs, including modest wages to prisoners, but returned a profit of $567,698 in the second year."[41] Yet, with the exception of federal institutions, the success of the PRIA and state governments to foster productive prison industries was questionable. "Several states did organize industrial corporations comparable to that of the federal system, but idleness continued to blight most prisons until the outbreak of World War II created a new demand."[42] Indeed, with the country mobilized under the "war effort," opposition to prison industries softened. Under Federal Prison Industries Inc., the corporation's 21 plants had dramatically increased output to the point where Bennett characterized them as "small war plants."[43] An executive order by the President in 1942 even permitted state facilities to compete for military contracts. Yet with the end of the war, such contracts came to an end, and with them most of the productive output of prison industries.

Following the war, the prison populations of the United States began to swell once more. Between 1945 and 1955, the rate per 100,000 of the state and federal prison population rose from 100.1 to 113.0; nearly a 22 percent increase.[44] Overcrowding and dilapidated facilities, some a century old, created intolerable conditions. In the early 1950s a series of riots rocked the nation's prisons. From Washington state to Michigan, New Jersey, California, and Massachusetts, prison uprisings challenged authority and order. In Ohio, a 1953 riot at Columbus eventually resulted in an $8,500,000 appropriation from the legislature to turn a reformatory into a medium-secure facility in an effort to relieve overcrowding.[45]

Indeed, the state prison system became quite costly. Between 1945 and 1955, expenditures by state governments for correctional facilities, in real dollars, rose from 82 to 268 million. With the addition of local and federal expenditures for corrections, the United States spent some 463 million dollars on such facilities in 1955.[46] And those prison industries that were operating by this time hardly began to offset such costs. In sum, despite the unusual conditions present during World War II, prison industries never recovered from the restrictive legislation enacted during the early decades of the century. The vast majority of inmates were left not only idle and unproductive, but a potential threat to the order of the institution as well.

The Juvenile Court and the Penetration of the Family

The situation in juvenile correctional institutions was not much better. As indicated in the previous chapter, the juvenile court in the United States had emerged as part of the specializing and segregating state care and control apparatus during the turn of the century. By Progressive design, the court was intended to provide individual care and attention to the child in trouble and to act in that child's best interest. The state, for its part, went along with the court's creation because Progressives argued – as they had justified the adoption of specialized institutions – that the new system would ensure a more exacting process of reformation. It was then, as John Sutton has characterized it, an "institutional compromise" between law and social welfare.[47] Thus the juvenile court would separate children from the corrupting influence of their association with adults and play an instrumental part in their adopting an "honest livelihood and to become of use to society instead of an injury to it."[48]

However, like many of the policies on the Progressive agenda, the juvenile court never quite measured up to its vision and, once again, the gap between rhetoric and reality was wide. The juvenile court's most fundamental contradiction was located within its two basic goals: to serve the interest of the child and, at the same time, be an agent of social control for the community and the state. As the critical literature which emerged in the 1960s and 1970s demonstrated, the court never really attained either of these goals. Children were never afforded the "special" treatment envisioned for them under *parens patriae*, nor were they provided the due process rights of adult proceedings. The result was a system of little care, little justice, and plenty of institutionalization.

The darker side of the reform story, therefore, was the regulation of family life by the state, and few alternatives to an institutional response to youthful misconduct. By 1940, juvenile courts in the United States handled 200,000 delinquency cases alone, not including the dependent and neglected – a rate of 10.5 per 1,000 of those between the ages of ten and 17. By 1955, the corresponding figures were 431,000 with a rate per 1,000 of 21.4.[49] In comparing figures from the US Bureau of the Census for juvenile correctional facilities between 1923 and 1950, we see that these populations rose from 27,238 in 1923, to 30,496 in 1933, and to 40,880 by 1950. The corresponding rates per 100,000 of those in the population under 18 years old were 65.7, 72,3, and 88.8 respectively.[50]

In sum, not unlike their adult counterparts, juvenile correctional agencies were more efficient at *collecting* offenders than they were at transforming them into model citizens. Indeed, as two critics would later state: "The rate of failure from our fixed institutions for young and old offenders has remained more constant through the years than any other index upon which we rely – cost of living, Dow Jones, or the annual precipitation of rain. An average of the recidivism rates reported by the most reliable researchers runs consistently in the range from one-half to two-thirds."[51] It would appear that public correctional facilities contributed heavily to America's growing population of institutionalized citizens.

Finally, in addition to the primary care and control facilities in the mental health and correctional systems, other more specialized facilities such as homes for the mentally retarded and physically handicapped, for the aged, for dependent and neglected youth, for unwed mothers, detention homes, and tuberculosis hospitals, all contributed to a tremendous growth in institutionalized populations. For example, between 1936 and 1954 the number of persons in public institutions for the mentally retarded rose from 92,572 to 136,926, or at a rate per 100,000 from 78 to 93.[52] Thus by 1950, according to the US Bureau of the Census, there were 1,566,846 persons in institutions or 1035.4 per 100,000 citizens.[53]

While it would be unwise to attempt to make specific statements concerning changes in the overall rate of institutionalization in the United States through the mid-twentieth century (given the less systematic nature of earlier surveys as well as changes in institutional categories), it seems fair to say that the number of incarcerated individuals increased considerably during the period. In addition, it is possible to outline changes within specific age groups. For those aged 65 and over for example, the rate per 100,000 of those in the almshouse, asylums, and feeble-minded facilities in 1923 was 1,555. By 1950, however, the rate for this age group in homes for the aged, asylums, and chronic hospitals was estimated at 3,135 – double the 1923 rate.[54]

Even considering the potential unreliability of early census data, these figures indicate the degree of America's substantial commitment to centralized, public institutions in confronting problems of care and control. But as I will demonstrate in chapters to come, a qualitatively different kind of state apparatus begins to evolve in the late 1950s and early 1960s, reflecting fundamental changes in the form and function of the American Liberal Welfare state.

5

Contradictions and Consequences in Post-war Psychiatry

As I have demonstrated in the previous chapter, by the mid-twentieth century, the use of public institutions as a means of caring for and controlling troublesome individuals in our society was at its zenith. Yet, something went awry. Every year, thousands of people entered these facilities; many of them never returned, and those that did were never quite the same. The conditions and consequences of these "out of sight, out of mind" places began to creep into the public consciousness. Prisons exploded in violent outbursts while haunting *exposés* revealed the back wards of the state hospitals for what they were: dens of human misery and neglect. Moreover, academicians began to question the very logic upon which these houses of therapy and correction were based. As Andrew Scull has stated, the defects thought to be uncovered "were not simply the consequence of administrative lapses or the lack of adequate funds, but rather . . . they reflected fundamental and irremediable flaws in the basic structure of such places."[1]

In addition to this powerful ideological movement was the fact that the use, or more accurately abuse, of incarceration had become extremely problematic for state governments. Thus we see that by the mid 1950s, the state hospital was not only the largest public care and control institution, but it would also become the site of the first *reduction* in the inmate population of a primary social control institution in the contemporary period.

I present evidence, some previously unexamined, to suggest that initial efforts by officials to reduce state hospital populations were prompted by (1) the apparent failure of the institution to return people to productive lives, (2) a concern for the impact of current and future fiscal expenditures if inmate populations continued to rise, and (3) the necessity for state managers to respond to the criticisms of reformers and the public over the intolerable conditions present in the institutions. Yet these initial moves toward reducing state hospital populations had a relatively minor impact on both the yearly census of patients and the organizational legitimacy of the asylums. It was not until a policy of "deinstitutionalization" and the provision of community-based care was articulated at the national level that a massive depopulation of the hospitals occurred.

The State Hospital in the "New Age" of Community Mental Health

As I have indicated, the first evidence of the movement towards "deinstitutionalization" or the reduction of institutionalized persons from state facilities in the contemporary period occurred in the state and county mental hospitals. After decades of yearly increases of as many as 10,000 patients a year, the population in these institutions, for the entire country, peaked in the year 1955 at 558,922. That year represented the culmination of the political, economic, and ideological viability of the state hospital, and set the stage for significant changes in the nature of contemporary care and control.

The idea of "community-based" prevention and treatment of mental illness had been around for some time, as this had been the goal of the early psychopathic hospitals. Yet as I have shown in previous chapters, these facilities were never an alternative care setting, they never challenged the legitimacy of the state hospital, and, in practice, they provided an organizational pathway to its wards. Why then did this strategy – the hallmark of the relatively unsuccessful turn of the century mental hygiene movement – become the centerpiece of post-war psychiatry and public policy? To answer this question, we must understand how a constellation of forces came to *reintro-*duce the possibility of "community care" while simultaneously undermining the role of the state hospital as an obsolete apparatus.

In the immediate post-war years, few spoke of reducing state hospital populations. Indeed, most discussions at that time emphasized institutional expansion and improvements to cope with chronic overcrowding and under-staffing. Literary *exposés* as well as newspaper and magazines articles chronicled the conditions of the state hospitals. These conditions were described by Dr Kenneth Appel, later president of the American Psychiatric Association, as "shocking, monstrous, and horrible;" he pointed out that the "grass surrounding the state hospital receives more care and consideration than the patients inside."[2] The benevolent, humane institution that Dorothea Dix had envisioned more than a century before was now subjected to the very criticism that she had levelled at the poorhouse and the prison.

Arguably the most powerful, if partial, statement on the conditions in public hospitals at that time was Albert Deutsch's *The Shame of the States*. Published in 1948, Deutsch's book, a collection of popular press articles, provided descriptive accounts and photographs of the author's visits to a number of state hospitals, revealing the bleakness of institutional life. Deutsch summed up the state of mental health care in the United States in this way:

> The American Psychiatric Association has established a set of minimum standards for mental hospitals. It says there should be at least one psychiatrist for every 30 patients, in certain types of mental diseases, and at least one for every 200 in others ... There should be at least one graduate nurse for every 40 patients ... [and] ... one attendant for every eight patients. At least $5 a day should be expended for the care and treatment of each patient. (The per capita

daily cost in state mental hospitals in 1946 averaged less than $1.25.) . . .

Not a single state mental hospital in the United States meets, or has ever met, even the minimum standards set by the APA in all major aspects of care and treatment!

In his concluding remarks, Deutsch sets out, in classical Progressive fashion, the characteristics of "the ideal state mental hospital," which is a better funded, well staffed, cheerful "therapeutic community with the single goal of helping patients recover."[3]

The call for reform and the ever-rising appropriations to the state hospitals prompted the participants of the forty-first annual meeting of the Governors' Conference in June 1949 to adopt a resolution stating that

Mental hygiene and the care and treatment of the mentally ill create some of the most important social and financial problems confronting the states today. In order that the states may be enabled to deal adequately with these problems, much additional information is needed with respect to personnel, administrative practices, and physical equipment.[4]

The Conference called on the Council of State Governments (CSG) to conduct the study and, one year later, the Council released a report entitled *Mental Health Programs of the Forty-eight States*. Along with its companion volume, *Training and Research in State Mental Health Programs*, published in 1953, these reports remain two of the most comprehensive assessments of the public mental health system in the immediate post-war period.[5] Moreover, the reports and opinions contained in the archives of both the Governors' Conference and the CSG represent an important part of understanding the collective interests and policies pursued by the state managers during the period of the mid and late 1950s.

While framed in optimistic language, in actuality, the CSG's reports present a relatively bleak picture of the state of public mental hospitals and – unless something could be done about the situation – increasingly poor prospects for the future. The CSG estimated that between 1880 and 1940 while general population had increased 2.6 times, the population of mental hospitals had risen 12.6 times. Further, less than half of the patients admitted to the hospitals were released within five years. In the year of the first report, there were just over 500,000 patients in the hospitals. The CSG went on to state that

> Between 1903 and 1948 the total growth in resident population of all mental hospitals was 406,474 patients. Of this growth, 84 percent was represented by the growth of state mental hospitals. The hospitalization rate of state mental hospitals has increased from 159.1 in 1903 to 323.1 in 1948. During that period, resident population of state hospitals increased by an annual average of 7,582. However, the annual increase has been somewhat greater in the past decade averaging 8,493 per year since 1938.[6]

The CSG would later estimate that the population, if unchecked could reach 600,000 by 1960.[7]

To what factors did the CSG attribute this dramatic rise? Convinced that mental illness was no more prevalent than one hundred years earlier, the CSG cited

1 "The growing willingness among families to send a mentally ill member to the hospital instead of taking care of him at home," the reasons being (a) city families have "a decreasing number of rooms," (b) "the absence during the day of other family members" and (c) "the objections of other residents in the community."

2 "More psychiatric hospitals are now located near urban centers, and more adequate hospital accommodations are available."

3 "The public is increasingly disposed to regard the care of the mentally ill as the responsibility of the state rather than that of the family."

4 "The stigma previously placed on admission to a mental hospital has declined."

5 "The ever rising proportion of the aged entering the hospitals due to the extension of the life span and the accompanying onset of senility and associated disorders." And

6 "The ability and willingness of physicians, teachers, social workers and the like to identify and refer individuals for symptoms of psychological distress."[8]

The cost of this care in the state hospitals, according to the CSG, "runs into significant amounts, and an analysis turns out to be a grim story. The burden, in many cases, is impoverishing the community, while in others so little has been spent that standards of care must surely be low."[9] Observing that state hospital appropriations rank as one of the "big four" among state government expenditures (the others include schools, social welfare, and highways), the CSG noted that the sums for the construction, maintenance, and operations of state hospitals were financed almost exclusively from state revenues. The report provides data from a survey of 37 states indicating that expenditures, in real dollars, for 1939 for both capital and maintenance, had been $110,208,242; by 1949 they were $359,466,689, and by 1950 appropriations for the state hospitals were $477,175,361.[10]

Information provided by 31 of the 37 states surveyed indicated that salaries and wages were the largest portion of the maintenance component of these years (54.6, 57, and 61.7 percent respectively), rising nearly 16 percent between 1949 and 1950 alone. Per patient cost for total maintenance expenditures, in real dollars for the reporting states, rose from a median of $245.90 in 1939 to $636.03 in 1949, $745.00 in 1950, and an estimated $789.00 for 1951. The report summarized per patient costs as having increased "tremendously since 1939" and were "still moving upward."[11]

These data presented to the Governors' Conference painted a grim picture of the long-term prospects for the state hospital. The Report of 1950 presents 40 recommendations, including first, that "adequate hospital space should be provided promptly."[12] Moreover, additional professional personnel, better services, organization, administration and accounting, and more specialized training and research were needed to transform the state hospital, while the additional development of mental health clinics would

> contribute to mental health generally and should enable hospitals to expand their convalescent leave and discharge programs to a much greater extent. It seems that much greater use could be made of such facilities to the great advantage of the community and the patient, since clinical and community care is much more economical than institutional treatment.[13]

Essentially, the CSG's recommendations follow the adage that one has to spend money in order to save money. Through prevention, research, and more efficient state hospitals, the states could reduce their mental health burden, i.e. halt or reverse the spiraling growth of the state hospital.

One would expect that the time necessary to establish and implement a comprehensive realignment of mental health policy would be considerable, let alone see the appearance of any "results." Yet somehow, almost mysteriously according to a later CSG report, by 1956 34 states had either stabilized or reduced the resident population of their mental hospitals. The CSG stated in their report of April 1958 that the trend was particularly spectacular when viewed against

> the fact that first admissions in 1956 were at their highest point in history . . . Insufficient evidence was at hand to establish accurately the reason for the decline in resident hospital populations. Mental hospital administrators as well as legislators and other state officials were perplexed as to whether the phenomenon was temporary or indicative of a future trend.[14]

The report offers these factors as possible explanations:

1   The new "wonder" drugs for "preparing hundreds of formerly 'hopeless' patients for treatment and improvement," admitting, however, that the drugs alone cannot have been responsible since their introduction occurred while "other elements were beginning to pay off."
2   A "growing recognition that a hospital's social environment has therapeutic qualities and that it can have curative effects."
3   "An increasing number of people with mental illnesses are being treated successfully in clinics while living at home and working in the community."
4   Early diagnosis "taking place more intensively and thoroughly, resulting in early treatment and in many cases avoiding the need for later hospitalization."
5   "Increased use of 'bridging' devices between hospital and community has permitted many patients, who were able to adjust well in hospital but feared to leave, to prepare gradually for normal community life."
6   Increased hospital personnel "so that more intensive treatment has been possible."
7   Increased use of general hospital wards providing community based treatments.[15]

However, there are considerable problems with these "explanations" for the origins of contemporary deinstitutionalization. The "wonder drug" answer, destined to be the most commonly cited, has been shown to be at best questionable, at worst, seriously flawed.[16] For example, inter-state as well as international variation in both decarceration trends and the introduction of psychoactive drugs indicates that the two were not temporally synchronized. In California for example, hospital populations continued to rise until 1960 despite the fact that the state hospitals were experimenting with drugs as early as 1953.[17] In France, hospital populations did not fall until the 1970s even though it was a French firm that pioneered the drugs in the first place, 20 years before.

Explanations (2) and (6) imply that the hospitals were, quite suddenly, providing a considerably better level of care and hence increasing their "cure" rate.[18] There is little to support this contention. For example, if in 1955 the states had spent even the $5.00 per diem standard set by the APA in the 1940s, the cost of that year would have been $1,020,032,650! In actuality, the states spent $627,470,000 in current dollars for operating expenditures that year.[19] While the states did increase spending and bed space during the 1950s, previous levels were sometimes so low that even modest increases may have tripled appropriations. Thus, many facilities never reached even the $5.00 per diem and were still considered overcrowded at the decade's end.[20] Indeed, given the actual financial commitments of the states, and the lack of any major breakthrough in the treatment of mental illness during the time period (with the exception of limited drug experimentation) it seems unlikely that the hospitals were suddenly transformed into models of therapeutic efficiency.

Finally, factors 3, 4, 5 and 7 offered by the CSG for decreasing populations are hardly explanations of both increasing releases *and* admissions. Rather, if the relatively few community treatment programs in existence were so effective at preventing hospitalization, admissions would have fallen instead of risen. Moreover, in its earlier reports, the CSG offered some fairly insightful reasons for the rise in hospital populations: urbanization, changes in family life, the objections of community residents, the expectation of state rather than family responsibility, and the extension of the life span. Yet now, in the rhetoric of "community care" these very factors were completely ignored. Somehow now the family and the community became receptive, and reintegration was not a problem.

Rather than some unexplained phenomenon or statistical quirk, the decline in hospital populations in 1956 was the result of a strategy of increasing releases nationwide. Between 1953 and 1954 net releases increased by 5 percent; between 1955 and 1956 they increased by 13 percent.[21] As two contemporary analysts put it, this first stage of deinstitutionalization represented a "phase-down that led to the opening of the back doors of these institutions for the release of long-stay patients and for the early discharge of newly admitted patients."[22] What the

CSG had left out of its "explanations" was the fact that on February 9, 1954 at the National Governors' Conference on Mental Health in Detroit, the Governors adopted a ten-point program, which would become, according to the CSG itself, a "guide for action in practically every state." The first proposal stated that "Psychiatric treatment with the fullest use of existing knowledge can return many more people to productive and useful lives. Increased appropriations for additional qualified mental health personnel . . . and intensive treatment programs should be provided by states at their next legislative sessions *to increase the number of patients discharged from state mental hospitals*" (emphasis added).[23] The remaining points of the document go on to stress the importance of training, research, and prevention in "the ultimate reduction" of the "serious accumulation of patients and costs" in the state hospitals. It would appear that, given the dramatic increase in releases reflected in the 1956 data, the ten-point program became a mandate for the Governors and legislatures to reduce hospital populations regardless of the actual implementation of "intensive treatment programs."

Opening the Back Doors: The Political Legitimacy of State Governments and the Early Signs of Deinstitutionalization

I began this section by stating in order to understand the *re*introduction of the notion of "community care" in the 1950s, it was necessary to uncover the political and economic forces, given the changing historical context, which were undermining the role of the state hospital. Factors consistent with my theoretical model provide for such an interpretation. First, attention focused on the hospitals by reformers and the media prompted state managers, who had basically paid little attention to the institution, to take a closer look at its conditions and future prospects. Investigations by agencies such as the Council on State Governments revealed that the facilities had an abysmal record at providing even a minimum of custodial care, let alone returning patients to "productive" lives. Moreover, data presented to the Governors' Conference demonstrated that the hospitals were consuming an ever-increasing portion of state budgets and, left unchecked, could evolve into fiscal sink-holes. During the conservative Eisenhower years, this regime attempted to curtail the expansion of federal participation in welfare services and shift the burden back to state governments. Federal aid to states for health care, for example, peaked in 1952 at $191,700,000, falling to a low of $124,900,000 in 1955, and not recovering to 1952 levels until the end of the decade. Meanwhile, the size of state governments grew at an alarming rate. Expenditures by state and local governments, as a percentage of GNP, had risen from 4.5 in 1947 to 7.1 in 1957. The number of employees at this level of government grew from 4,285,000 in 1950 to 6,088,000 in 1959 with the payroll for the period rising from $915,000,000 to $2,042,000,000.[24] Clearly, state governments were facing pressures for fiscal conservatism, if expenditures continued to rise at similar rates. On the other hand, officials simply could not permit the conditions that existed in the state hospitals to continue.

State managers were left with the choice of doing nothing, with the probability of facing an ever-rising population of patients, spiraling costs (even at sub-standard funding levels), and the possibility that the custodial conditions might evolve into a real political liability, revealing officials as inhumane and incompetent. On the other hand, they could continue to support the institution and follow the recommendations consistent with advancing the quality of care in the hope that "intensive treatment" programs and prevention strategies would be successful at curing patients, while at the same time, risking both fiscal collapse and their political legitimacy. Finally, state governments could abandon the institution since shutting the doors would ease the fiscal and administrative burden. Yet such an action would be sure to create a political backlash in local communities (both in those that relied on the economic boon of the hospitals and those where ex-patients might be placed) and thus more problems than would be solved.

Looking back, it would appear that the states began the last alternative, in the guise of the second. Not that they had any intention at that time of closing the hospitals; rather that their actions initiated the movement away from the hospital, fostering the notion of "community care." The beginning "phasedown" had crucial advantages. First, increasing releases reduced overcrowding and eased criticisms, while it increased per patient costs (even if funding levels remained the same); thus administrators appeared to be making headway in addressing the problems of the state hospitals as well those of mental illness in general. Moreover, once the hospital census peaked in 1955, the subsequent reductions in their population was used to justify quickly cancelling costly building projects.

For example, the Council on State Governments report for 1958–9 pointed out that, "Although measures to alleviate overcrowding still are mandatory in a few states, capital outlay expenditures in some are being reduced in the current biennium. This reflects the continued leveling off of patient population."[25] Finally, by increasing rates of first admissions and readmissions as well as releases, the social control function of the state hospital remained intact, while yearly censuses could be reduced. "As long as revolving-door patients could be easily returned to these hospitals – by families, local agencies, or police authorities – deinstitutionalization was not a major political issue."[26]

Community Psychiatry and the "New Frontier" of Progressive Social Reform

In December of 1960, the Joint Commission on Mental Illness and Health, an interdisciplinary body created under the Mental Health Study Act of 1955, presented its final report to the US

Congress. The document, entitled *Action for Mental Health*, became the centerpiece for an emerging national mental health policy.[27] Not unlike previous assessments of mental health care in the United States, *Action for Mental Health* argued for substantial increases in basic research, training, and services. Recommending that current expenditures be doubled in five years and tripled in ten – with the Federal government assuming a "major share" of such costs – the report proposed that the treatment of the acute mentally ill take place in Community Mental Health Clinics (one for every 50,000 citizens), in General Hospital Psychiatric Wings located in "every community," and in Intensive Psychiatric Clinics created from the conversion and/or creation of "smaller state hospitals, of 1,000 beds or less and suitably located for regional service." Chronically ill patients, the report contended, should be cared for in "chronic disease centers" (not specific to mental illness), which would be supplemented with "aftercare, intermediate care, and rehabilitative services."[28]

In addition to the influence of the Joint Commission, which was dominated by members of the American Psychiatric Association and the American Medical Association's Council on Mental Health, a mental health lobby had emerged during the period.[29] Centered on the National Institute of Mental Health as its primary governmental body, this group of reformers, professional association members, interested politicians, and the like, pushed for mental health reform. The lobby itself was fragmented into two groups, however. According to David Mechanic there were

> those psychiatrists with a public health viewpoint, who wished to develop completely new precedents for mental patient care, and those psychiatrists more within the medical model, who felt that considerable federal assistance should be invested in improving the quality of mental hospitals and their capacities to provide adequate treatment to patients. Those who favored a more radical break with the past system of providing mental health services through state and federal hospitals were more influential

with President Kennedy, and the final decision was to give greatest impetus to the community health centers.[30]

Indeed, Kennedy claimed that "the time has come for a bold new approach" to the treatment of mental illness, and he introduced a planned federal initiative to Congress in February 1963. After a series of relatively uneventful hearings, the Community Mental Retardation and Community Mental Health Centers Construction Act (CMHCC) was later passed into law on October 31, 1963 (PL-88-164).[31] The Act authorized funds ($150 million over the next three years), for the construction of "community-based" mental health centers. The facilities were charged with providing inpatient and outpatient services, partial hospitalization, and emergency or "crisis" services to specific geographical locales or "catchment" areas of up to 200,000 people. The appropriations were intended (or at least maneuvered through Congress) as "seed" money to help the states shift the locus of the treatment of mental illness from the state hospitals to the community. Kennedy claimed on signing the bill into law that, "Under this legislation, custodial mental institutions will be replaced by therapeutic centers. It should be possible, within a decade or two, to reduce the number of patients in mental hospitals by 50 percent or more. The new law provides the tools with which we can accomplish this."[32]

To this time, reduction in the state hospital population had been relatively minor. In this "phase-down" period, between 1955 and 1965, the hospital census was reduced from 558,922 to 475,202, about 15 percent, or from 344.4 per 100,000 to 247.6.[33] In the post-1965 period however, important legislation accelerated deinstitutionalization. In 1965, an amendment to the 1963 CMHCC Act provided for the staffing grants left out of the original bill. The Social Security Amendments Act of 1965 enacted Medicare and Medicaid programs that included coverage for inpatient hospital care for the mentally ill and skilled nursing home care. Later in 1972, additional Social Security Amendments, specifically the creation of the Supplemental Security Income (SSI) program, replaced state sharing for the totally and permanently disabled with 100 percent federal assistance. The effect of these legislative actions was to provide fiscal incentive to states to deinstitutionalize patients under their responsibility and shift patient support to the federal level, which was only provided if the person lived "in the community."

Moreover, during this period a powerful ideological movement concerning patients' rights emerged which challenged, through legal and political mechanisms, the dominance of psychiatrists, hospital staff and administrators over the lives and treatment of the mentally ill. Between the mid-1960s and 1970s, case litigation was filed on behalf of hospital patients concerning their right to receive and refuse treatments, the right to privacy, the guarantee of a "least-restrictive environment," the provision of wages for labor performed and, most importantly, the right to due process in commitment proceedings. These legal precedents, particularly those concerning the power of the state to involuntarily commit an individual to a hospital, contributed to a decline in the use of institutionalization.

Thus, during this second phase of deinstitutionalization (post-1965), the states experienced dramatic reductions in the census of state hospitals. Between 1965 and 1980, the population in these facilities fell from 475,202 to 156,482 or at a rate per 100,000 of 247.6 to 70.2.[34] In 1955, 77 percent of all mental health care episodes occurred on an inpatient basis while nearly two-thirds of these episodes occurred in state and county mental hospitals. By 1975, inpatient care episodes had been reduced to 27 percent with only one-third of these occurring in state hospitals,[35] while comparisons between the states indicate considerable variation in the pace and rate of deinstitutionalization.[36] These national data demonstrate that the movement away from the state hospital was indeed a widespread and pervasive trend, encompassing what one group of authors called "one of the most tumultuous and far-reaching periods of change in the history of mental health care in the United States."[37] In the next chapter I explore some of the factors that brought about this powerful change.

6

Public Policy under the Liberal Welfare State

One of the first attempts to understand the more recent deinstitutionalization movement from a political-economic perspective was Andrew Scull's *Decarceration*.[1] In this work, Scull attempts to peel away the ideological rhetoric of "community treatment" and reveal the materialist roots of the movement. Adapting the principles of James O'Connor's "fiscal crisis" thesis, Scull argued that modern, segregative modes of social control had become "social expenses," constantly outstripping the state's ability to afford them.[2] While Scull's book was instrumental in fostering the theoretical shift towards considering "the state" in the analysis of the transformation of social control policies, the debates it has sparked have raised numerous questions concerning both the theoretical and empirical "fit" of the analysis. Thus a number of important aspects of Scull's thesis remain problematic. For example, was there indeed a "fiscal crisis" stimulating the initial moves toward deinstitutionalization or were the 1950s a time of prosperity rather than shortages? What levels of the state were affected? What prompted the federal government to take on a national mental health policy in the early 1960s? Would, and in reality did, decarceration save money? Was it really intended to be more economical in the first place?

The evidence I have presented in the previous chapter does suggest that *state* governments were under substantial pressure, on the one hand, to eradicate the scandalous conditions of the state hospitals, and on the other, to reduce both the short term, and certainly the potential long-term fiscal drain of the hospitals. Given the actual number of discharges in concert with rising admission rates, the "phase-down" strategies pursued by the states initially had a relatively minor impact on the organizational legitimacy of the hospitals. It was not, however, until the federal government intervened in the early 1960s and formally articulated a national community mental health policy that accelerated deinstitutionalization occurred. It is imperative that any state-centered analysis should come to grips with the dynamics of this intervention, locating it within the broader interests of the state at that time. Central to such an understanding is a consideration of the strategies of both the Kennedy and Johnson administrations.

From the "New Frontier" to the "Great Society": The Politics and Policies of the Kennedy-Johnson Years

When the Kennedy administration took office in 1961 unemployment was at seven percent, for the fourth year in a row the annual rate was more than five percent, and the economy was at the bottom of a recession having suffered lagging growth since the mid 1950s.[3] After a somewhat hesitant beginning, the President and his advisors launched a program which has come to be considered the pinnacle of America's "fiscal revolution."[4] Embodied in the "new economics," the administration pursued, unlike any before it, a Keynesian macroeconomic policy of employing discretionary fiscal strategies to stabilize and expand the economy: (1) There was a new emphasis on and quantification of the goal of full employment. (2) The goals of full employment and of growth were tied together by emphasizing the related concepts of "potential output" and the "gap." (Potential output is the output that can be obtained at full employment, the gap is the measure of output not produced when unemployment exceeds four percent.) And finally, the main objective of macroeconomic policy was expressed in "closing the gap."[5] Once the gap was closed and full employment obtained, the increased tax revenues provided for "fiscal dividends" in the form of increased government expenditures for society or in tax reductions. Before any of this could happen, however, the economy had to expand; thus economic "growth" became the "supreme, number one priority," of the Kennedy administration.[6]

Kennedy and his advisors attempted to "close the gap" by spurring initial economic growth through a combination of government spending and tax reduction. With the aid of a cooperative Federal Reserve Board which permitted the money supply to rise with spending, and with relatively stable prices and wages due in part to the administration's "guideposts" governing fluctuations, Kennedy set about stimulating both private business investment and personal consumption. At first, deficit government spending was employed. According to Robert Gordon, between "the first quarters of 1961 and 1962, federal spending on goods and services expanded by $6.5 billion, well over twice the increase during the preceding year."[7] While there was some evidence of recovery, business investment was lagging and the administration took to tax reduction. This resulted in the Revenue Act of 1962 which, in contradiction to its title, provided business with an investment tax credit. A second tax reduction in 1964 provided for regressive personal and corporate income tax cuts. One estimate put the eventual contribution of this tax reduction to the gross national product at about $36 billion.[8] By 1965, the target four percent unemployment was met. Moreover, as Gordon put it, "the early and mid-1960s were a profitable period for American business, and rising profits created a business climate favorable to the investment boom that got underway in late 1963."[9] By 1965, the "new economics" was triumphant in "closing the gap."

The macroeconomic strategy initiated by the Kennedy administration has important implications for understanding the context of this regime's social policies and, in particular, the deinstitutionalization movement. On the ideological level, the

notion of "community" mental health appealed to the administration because it offered an apparent new direction for policy –
a break with the past – one part of the expanding "new frontier"
of progressive social reform. But the policy also meshed
with the administration's macroeconomic objectives as well.
First, the training, staffing, construction and provision of
community mental health provided a mechanism for injecting
federal dollars into the economy. And once a full employment
economy was obtained, "fiscal dividends" would pay for the
expanding network of community mental health facilities.
Secondly, a basic premise of the decarceration movement was
that people could now lead "productive" lives in the community. Once released from an institution, an individual is now a
consumer of goods and services – a key element of economic
exchange – and of the administration's strategy of economic
stimulation.

Even if a person is solely supported by public sector funds in
"the community" rather than in an institution, those funds are
diverted back into the economy through the consumption of
housing, food and other basic necessities, thus ensuring private
sector accumulation and investment. For those unable to take
care of themselves, the provision of "community" organizations such as nursing homes, board and care establishments and
the like, provided another source of expenditures targeted at
private accumulation. This is *not* to say that this was the sole
motivation behind the administration's social policies. Rather,
the point is that in considering an array of options in specific
policy areas, the administration was predisposed to pursue
policies that were consistent with its broader objectives. Thus,
from the federal administration's point of view, it was not so
much that deinstitutionalization would save money (although
that is the way it was presented to fiscal conservatives), rather it
was the way in which the monies were spent.

Finally, upper-middle-class liberal activists and their political
allies, one segment of the post-New Deal Democratic party that
swept Kennedy into power, seized the availability of federal
"grants-in-aid" to local governments "to extend their control
over the policies, programs, and hiring practices of municipal

agencies."[10] These federal officials were then able to use bureaucratic goods and services to reach local, predominantly urban, minority constituents, circumventing and/or forcing municipal departments to conform to Washington's mandate. Once set in motion by the Kennedy administration, these principles were carried through during the Johnson years with the "Great Society" programs. As I have outlined above, important legislation such as the amendments to the Social Security Act in 1965 accelerated public decarceration by providing the incentives to the states to transfer fiscal responsibility to the federal government who was willing to pay for "community" care.

Yet, things turned sour for the "new economics." The Johnson administration's decision to escalate US involvement in Southeast Asia dramatically increased federal spending for military hardware at the same time that the expansionary tax reduction strategies of the earlier years were still in place. The added expenditures had the affect of "over-heating" the economy producing tremendous inflationary pressures. "Fiscal dividends" were being disproportionately absorbed by military expenditures. Moreover, Johnson's war effort alienated the liberal wing of the Democratic party, creating a power struggle that ultimately undermined the party's own coalitional base. In order to halt rising inflation, the Nixon administration instituted restrictive fiscal actions when it came into power. The rate of government spending was attacked, the investment tax credits initiated by Kennedy and Johnson were cancelled, scheduled reductions in excise taxes were postponed, and a tax surcharge was extended until the end of 1968.[11] In addition, the Federal Reserve Board began tightening the money supply. In combination, these fiscal policies brought on a recession in 1970. During these deflationary times, business profits fell, unemployment rose, and increased transfer payments pushed the federal budget into debt.

In summary, at the level of *state* government, initial efforts at deinstitutionalization were prompted, in part, by a threatening "fiscal crisis." Yet in Scull's analysis, we leap from the budgetary constraints of the states in the 1950s to the full-blown "fiscal crisis" of the federal state in the 1970s. The intervening history, however, is critical to a complete understanding of the period. At the federal level, the Kennedy administration's response to a recessionary economy was to *increase* rather than cut government spending, in an effort to stimulate economic growth. The aim of this Keynesian macroeconomic policy was to encourage both private investment/profitability and consumer demand. Yet the political and economic climate changed dramatically during the decade. Not only did Kennedy's "fiscal dividends" not appear until 1965, but they were quickly siphoned off by Johnson's war effort and the ensuing inflationary spiral. The Nixon administration, attempting to cope with these changing economic times, was both ideologically and fiscally conservative in its response. As David Mechanic put it, "Not only was the administration unsympathetic to mental health questions, but existing programs for mental health centers, research, research training, and professional manpower were phased down or out or allowed to erode with inflation."[12] Thus, by the 1970s, the "fiscal crisis" did appear at the federal level; further moves towards decarceration, as well as cuts in mental health appropriations in general, were intended to trim budgets. These conditions were not conducive to the evolution of even a basic public community mental health network,[13] and with the economic incentives in place, the private sector moved in further, filling the void left by the lack of public sector alternatives. Given that, in practice, "in the community" actually means that an individual more than likely now lived in an alternative institutional setting, one must characterize the public decarceration movement as at best, *trans*institutionalism. At its worst, the policy resulted in the severe neglect of those "dumped" on urban streets, left to survive in what Michael Dear and Jennifer Wolch have called "landscapes of despair."[14]

"Gray Gold": The New American Nursing Home Industry

Probably the most dramatic evidence of this transinstitutionalism is the growth of the nursing home industry. As we saw in previous chapters, the nursing home had its origins in the evolution of the public almshouse. Segregative modes of institutional social control and direct transfer payments to individuals had reduced the almshouse population to what the 1950 Census termed a "home for the aged." Although such homes had always been predominantly proprietary in nature, most were non-profit and/or small "family care" homes – barely considered commercial ventures – and the services provided were not reimbursable from the federal government.[15] In fact, in 1950, Congress attempted to encourage the growth of public facilities by making permissible the payment of Old Age Assistance (OAA) monies to public medical facilities and, later, in 1954 the Hill-Burton Hospital Construction Act was amended in order to provide funds for the construction of public, non-profit nursing homes.

However, in 1956, with the backing of the American Nursing Home Association, the Small Business Administration inaugurated a loan program for proprietary nursing homes. Three years later, mortgage guarantees for proprietary homes were made available by congress under the Federal Housing Authority (PL-86-372). By 1974, 110,485 nursing home beds had been constructed under this program. Other legislation such as the Kerr-Mills bill of 1960 created the Medical Assistance for the Aged, provided for skilled nursing care independent of OAA funds, and required that all institutions receiving vendor payments from the federal government meet the "medical institutions" definition. Finally, the Social Security Amendments of 1965 (Titles XIX and XVIII) created the Medicaid and Medicare programs which further encouraged the provision of proprietary care.[16]

These actions had the effect of severing the American nursing home from its public welfare past and transforming it into its present-day medicalized form. Moreover, it would appear beyond coincidence that this legislative activity took place during the same period that state and the federal government were decarcerating the state hospitals. As Paul Lerman noted of the trend, "In the late 1950s and early 1960s, entrepreneurial public officials, interested in depopulating the state mental hospitals created an extra source of demand for released geriatric patients. Nursing homes figured prominently in the plans of mental hospital after-care workers."[17] The growth of the nursing home industry between the 1950s and the 1980s has been staggering, reflecting both the transinstitutionalization of the geriatric mental patient and the political, fiscal, and social incentives to engage these facilities in providing long-term custodial care and control of the elderly. According to data from the National Center for Health Statistics, in 1963 there were 510,180 nursing home beds or 2.87 beds per 100 elderly over 65; by 1973 the figures were 1,107,258 and 6.1 respectively – an overall increase of 117 percent and an annual expansion rate of 8.1 percent. According to the 1980 US Census, there were 1.2 million people, 65 years and over, in nursing homes.[18]

According to the National Institute of Mental Health (NIMH), between 1960 and 1970 the percentage of elderly enumerated by the US census as being in mental hospitals decreased from about 30 percent to 12 percent, whereas the proportion in nursing homes during the same period rose from 63 to 82 percent. NIMH estimated in 1974 that more than half (58 percent) of nursing home residents have had a primary diagnosis of mental illness, thus making the nursing home the largest single site of care and control for such individuals.[19] Between 1969 and 1974, a National Center for Health Statistics (NCHS) study found a 48 percent increase in the number of nursing home residents with mental disabilities.[20] And in 1974 alone, 85,000 nursing home residents were transferred directly from mental hospitals. Moreover, the Nixon administration established a national goal to return one-third of the 200,000 mentally retarded in public facilities to "the community." In 1974, nursing homes received 26 percent of the 9,000 individuals released from 115 facilities that year.[21]

According to the US Health Care Financing Administration, Americans spent a little over $25 billion dollars for nursing home care for the elderly in 1984, 9.5 percent of the total spent on personal health. Moreover, nursing home expenditures increased at a rate of 17.4 percent between 1980 and 1981 and 12.9 percent between 1981 and 1982 – more rapidly than overall health care expenditures – and, given demographic predictions, the elderly will consume an increasing portion of America's health care dollar in the future.[22] And finally, in reference to the transinstitutionalization of the elderly mentally ill, nursing homes currently receive more than one-third of the expenditures for direct care of the mentally ill.[23]

More than 70 percent of all nursing beds are in for-profit homes and the private sector stands poised to capture this expansive market. So much so that one financial journal recently entitled an article on the industry, "Gray Gold."[24] Not unlike the health care system as a whole, the nursing home industry has been experiencing considerable consolidation and corporatization during the last decade.[25] Once dominated by small operators, nursing home "chains," a segment of the for-profit hospital management sector, now control close to 30 percent of all homes and 35 percent of all beds. As one financial analyst put it, "The smaller operators continue to be forced out of the industry at an accelerating rate. The economies of scale and efficient operating practices of the larger chains represent the only long-term answer to sustained profitability."[26] The largest, Beverly Enterprises (itself recently the victim of a corporate takeover bid), has grown almost exponentially through an aggressive program of acquisitions of smaller firms. In 1982, the firm held over 70,000 beds and projected to exceed 120,000 by 1985.

In addition to nursing homes, other privatized care and control facilities principally but not exclusively used by the elderly and disabled include those categorized as providing "domiciliary-care," or a limited amount of supervision, protection, and personal care, as opposed to the provision of skilled medical care. Such facilities include board and care homes, adult homes, shelter care facilities, group homes, and the like as well as some categories of single-room occupancies or SROs.[27] Given the limited licensing and reporting requirements, as well as the transient nature of these facilities, data on enumeration and organizational characteristics are limited. However, the data that are available indicate that these institutional types represent an important form of privatized "community care."

Since board and care type homes are ineligible to be classified as Medicare or Medicaid medical institutions, their income is derived from other third party sources, primarily under the federal Supplemental Security Income (SSI) program. In order to receive such funds a person must be psychiatrically certified as disabled. In a survey of five such facilities in California, 75 percent of the residents were recipients of SSI.[28] By extrapolating data provided to the Social Security Administration on SSI recipients, Lerman estimates that nationally, board and care inmates receiving SSI benefits number at least 360,000.[29] Phil Brown, citing a 1976 survey by NIMH, however, reports that a total of 1,075,900 residents (not only SSI recipients) in 15,737 facilities were enumerated, "excluding the lowest level of boarding homes."[30] Moreover, Brown also illustrates the utilization of single-room occupancies (SROs) in the New York City area, stating that the "city's Upper Westside contains an estimated 7,000 chronic patients living in SROs. Estimates of the citywide population of mentally ill persons in SROs range from 10,000 to 20,000."[31] Clearly, given the magnitude of the available estimates, these relatively new organizational forms have become a central feature of a post public deinstitutionalization and newly "privatized" social care and control system.

The Goal of "Reintegration": Offenders on Probation and Parole

The decarceration movement was not limited to the state mental hospitals. The ideological critique of the institution and the same political and economic forces were at work in the area of corrections as well. As I have shown in the previous chapter, correctional facilities, both adult and juvenile, experienced expansive population growth in the immediate post-war period. The 1950s were a time of overcrowding, prisoner uprisings, expanding budgets, and limited production in prison "industries." Between 1955 and 1961, the end-of-year census of prisoners in federal and state correctional institutions had increased from 185,780 to 220,149 or at a rate per 100,000 of 112 to 119. Yet in 1961 there was an abrupt reversal in the post-war pattern as the census fell to 117 per 100,000 and continued to decline each year until 1973 when the rate stood at 93.[32] What accounts for this turnaround? Had "crime" fallen as precipitously? It would appear not. Data from the Uniform Crime Reports covering the period 1957 to 1967 indicate that reported crimes, both violent and property offenses, more than doubled, climbing from 1,422,000 to 3,811,000 or at a rate per 100,000 of 835 to 1,926.[33] Moreover, during this time, the number of individuals arrested rose from 2,069,000 to 5,265,000.[34] Was the reduction in incarceration a function of a demographics – a decline in the population "at risk?" In fact, during the 1960s, the average annual percentage change in the population of individuals thought to be the most responsible for criminal activities, those between the ages of 15 and 29, was 3.41, making it the fastest growing segment of the population during the decade.[35]

In reality, the drop in prison populations in the early 1960s reflected the response of state legislatures and criminal justice officials who were faced with deteriorating institutions. Not unlike the conditions present in the state mental hospitals just a few years earlier, the country's prisons were overcrowded, physically dilapidated, and in need of expansive and expensive additions if trends continued unabated. Moreover, given the insurrections of the 1950s and increasing litigation filed by and on behalf of prisoners, the institution was well on its way to becoming extremely politicized.[36] And finally, not unlike the mental hospitals, the accumulation of inmates in prisons, and the apparent frequency with which they returned, provided clear evidence that the penal institution was failing to "rehabilitate" its charges. The US Bureau of Prisons summed up the situation in 1957 this way:

> Despite the expenditure of billions of dollars for law enforcement, for the operation of courts, and probation services, and for the institutional care of convicted offenders, prison populations continue to increase. Each year some 4,000 men and women are added to the population of the already overcrowded institutions for adult offenders throughout the United States. Some 70 percent of prisoners received in the state and federal institutions have served prior terms. Since the failure rate is so high and so costly, not only financially but in human terms, it is imperative that the major contributory factors be determined so that new programs may be devised and existing programs improved.[37]

Yet before any "new programs" were created, before any significant government funded, community-based correctional centers existed, state and federal officials began manipulating the system in order to depopulate the penitentiaries. Beginning in 1962, rather than accelerating parole releases many states simply stopped sending convicted criminals to prison; they started closing the front door. While parole releases remained fairly constant during the period, the number of prisoners received from court peaked in 1961 at 93,513 and fell to 79,351 by 1970.[38] Rather than "open the back door" as the mental hospitals had done, prison officials slowed the flow into the facilities and let the expiration of sentences reduce the census. This option was politically more viable since direct releases would have been available to the scrutiny of the media and the public.

Again, not unlike the deinstitutionalization of the mental hospitals, reductions in the adult prison population began with little ceremony. The movement was not prompted by any significant legislation or government action, and, just like the rise of the community mental health movement, the policy of

community corrections was never formally and governmental-
ly articulated until after the fact. The companion ideological
statement from corrections to *Action for Mental Health*, was the
Johnson Administration's *The Challenge of Crime in a Free
Society*, the report of the President's Commission on Law
Enforcement and Administration of Justice.[39] The emphasis on
"community-based" alternatives to the "debilitating effects of
the institution" pronounced by the Joint Commission were
echoed in the later volume:

> The task of corrections therefore includes building or
> rebuilding solid ties between the offender and the com-
> munity, integrating and reintegrating the offender into
> community life – restoring family ties, obtaining employ-
> ment and education, securing in a larger sense a place for
> the offender in the routine functioning of society . . . The
> goal of reintegration is likely to be furthered much more
> readily by working with offenders in the community than
> by incarceration. Additionally other goals are met. One is
> economy. In 1965 it cost, on the average, about $3,600 a
> year to keep a youngster in a training school, while it costs
> less than one-tenth that amount to keep him on
> probation.[40]

The Report itself is quite frank in pointing out that these
goals were somewhat *ad hoc*: "With two-thirds of the total
corrections caseloads under probation or parole supervision
today, the central question is no longer whether to handle
offenders in the community but how to do it safely and
effectively."[41] Talk of community-based corrections at the
federal level began during the Kennedy Administration,
although specific initiatives centered primarily on juvenile
justice (see below). In 1965 however, in anticipation of the
release of the President's Commission, congress passed the
Federal Prisoner Rehabilitation Act (18 US Code 4082) which
included provisions for "work-release, short-term furloughs,
and transfer of adult offenders to community treatment centers." Similar actions followed in many states.[42] In California,

for example, the state enacted the probation subsidy law of 1965 which provided financial inducements to local jurisdictions for not sending adults and juveniles to state institutions. The result: the proportion of superior court defendants sent to prison in the state dropped from 23.3 percent in 1965 to 9.8 percent in 1969.[43]

Changes in the juvenile justice system, as compared to adult corrections, were time-lagged. While the census of public, adult correctional facilities fell throughout the 1960s, juvenile facilities continued to grow. Between 1960 and 1970 the census of persons in training schools had risen from 45,695 to 66,457 or at a rate per 100,000 of 25.5 and 32.7 respectively.[44] Little governmental action, at the state or federal level, had been directed at reducing these populations. For example, during the Kennedy administration Congress passed the Juvenile Delinquency and Youth Offenses Act (PL-87-274) which contained the vague goal of providing the assistance in "developing techniques for the prevention and control of juvenile delinquency and youth offenses, and to encourage the coordination of efforts among governmental and nongovernmental . . . agencies concerned with such problems."

The President's Commission of 1967 found that the juvenile justice system was in need of serious reappraisal, noting that over 80 percent of all juvenile institutions were operating at or near capacity, that their populations were continuing to rise and that they were becoming increasingly expensive to operate. If this trend continued, the Commission estimated that the numbers of juveniles incarcerated could increase by as much as 70 percent by 1975.[45] However it was not until several amended versions of what would become the Juvenile Justice and Delinquency Prevention Act of 1974 (PL-93-415) that federal efforts would have an impact on public juvenile incarceration. The Act was designed to "prevent young people from entering our failing juvenile justice system, and to assist communities in developing more sensible and economical alternatives for youngsters already in the juvenile justice system."[46] The Act mandated that states pursue policies for the deinstitutionalization of youth, decriminalization (particularly of status-offenders), and diversion from the justice system for as many youths as possible.

The mandate embodied in this legislation, and the state sponsored versions that followed, has been most evident in admissions to public detention facilities, in particular in the treatment of status-offenders, and more specifically for females.[47] These facilities experienced a 14.6 percent decline in numbers of admissions between 1974 and 1979 or at a rate per 100,000 from 1791 to 1571, a 12.3 percent decline. Female admission to detention centers, in rates per 100,000 fell 37.6 percent between 1974 and 1979.[48] On the other hand, admissions to public juvenile training schools for the nation as a whole remained virtually unchanged during the period, moving from 226 per 100,000 in 1974 to 228 (again, if gender and offense are specified, female admissions for status-offenses fell quite dramatically). Census data for public training schools between 1974 and 1983, measured by one-day counts, rose modestly from 45,694 to 48,701. This trend occurred despite radical breaks with public juvenile correctional facilities such as the closing of all such institutions in the state of Massachusetts in the early 1970s. In summary, while efforts to deinstitutionalize adults from public correctional facilities during the 1960s were relatively successful, similar attempts to lessen the rate of incarceration for adolescents in public institutions during the 1970s were confined to restricting the involvement of status-offenders in the juvenile justice system. While their evolution followed different courses, these movements have ultimately contributed to the expanded role of private social control facilities in the 1980s.

Crises in the Community: the Politicization of America's "Crime Wave"

The depopulation of the country's adult prisons continued until 1973 when the census bottomed out at 196,092, at a rate per 100,000 of 93. By adopting an ideology of "community-based" corrections, federal and state officials had successfully headed off the massive administrative and financial expansion of prison bed space that would have been necessary had previous trends continued. Moreover, rather than simply halt the growth of prison populations, they actually reduced the number of charges under their control. Yet by the early 1970s, the political and social mood of America had begun to change. After a decade of civil disobedience, assassinations, political demands by minorities, a basically unpopular war, and changing social norms, the country's social order appeared, to many, to be on the verge of collapse. As Francis Cullen and Karen Gilbert characterized it, at that time, "'Crime' became a codeword for all that was wrong with American society, a symbol of disruptive forces that were undermining traditional patterns of authority and precipitating the decay of the social fabric."[49] Even those liberal politicians, academicians, and reformers who were once wedded to "progressive" penology seemed to all but abandon the cause, some even declared that "nothing works."[50] In Francis Allen's terms, we were witnessing the decline of "the rehabilitative ideal."[51]

In fact throughout the 1960s crime rates had continued to rise in almost incredible increments; evidence of America's continuing "crime wave." Dramatic media portrayals of crime and its victims amplified the call to "do something" and to "get tough" on law and order. In 1976, President Gerald Ford argued that the mandatory incarceration of felons was necessary to insure the "domestic tranquillity" of American society. The conservative backlash to the policies of the 1960s sent shock waves through the criminal justice system in the form of determinant sentencing, "tougher" sentences, and restitution, clogging court systems and, once again, increasing institutionalization. Between 1973 and 1984, the population in state and federal institutions climbed from 204,211 to 445,381 at a standardized rate from 96 to 188 – more than doubling both in absolute numbers and in rate during a ten-year period.[52]

In their effort to respond to the crisis of political legitimacy brought on by the "crime problem," state managers in the 1980s found themselves faced with yet again overcrowded, idle, expensive, and regularly explosive penal institutions. Confronted by historically high budget deficits and a public unyielding in its demands for the incarceration of offenders, legislators and correctional officials began seeking new ways of confronting this classic dilemma. Under the Reagan Administration, "private sector involvement" has become the rage in the corrections field, promising to be in the interest of all concerned.

In a report sponsored by the US Department of Justice entitled *The Privatization of Corrections*, the authors envision a "new" marriage between the public and private sectors in solving the problems of the justice system.[53] Three areas are explored: the participation of the private sector in prison work programs, the use of private sector alternatives for the financing and construction of prison facilities, and, finally, the use of private organizations to actually manage and operate correctional institutions. In rhetoric harking back to the early nineteenth century, a summary report states that prison industries are "the most logical place to find private sector involvement. A captive workforce, free use of space and utilities, and the opportunity to address a major social problem seem designed to satisfy both the entrepreneurial and public interests of the private sector."[54]

While proceeding with "guarded optimism," the report cites legal restrictions in some states founded on "union opposition and adverse public reactions," yet sees the movement "gaining momentum." Nineteen businesses are said to serve as the owner-operator, investor, or purchaser of one or more prison industries across the country including the Best Western hotel chain which has installed computer terminals in a women's facility in Arizona and has inmates making reservations. In California, Trans World Airlines has a similar system arranged at a juvenile facility.[55] During a recent labor dispute between TWA and its employees' union, inmates at the institution worked 12-hour shifts, and, in effect, were "scab" labor, undermining the union's bargaining position. In Florida, a prison industry program turned over management of 43 industries at 17 prisons to the private sector. A justice department consultant extolled the virtues of this system, stating that "Reduced idleness, better training and preparation for employment once they are released, and opportunities to repay victims and greater revenue for the state are anticipated benefits . . . This area of private sector participation may hold the greatest promise for introducing new models of corrections practice – models where entire prisons are organized around various industrial activities and work opportunities."[56]

Financing and lease/purchase options are currently being explored by a number of states and localities. Possibilities include the use of private sector monies instead of public tax funds for prison construction as well as the long-term leasing by the state of facilities which are funded and constructed with private sector money. With a projected $5 billion to be spent on prison expansion in the next decade, interest has been shown by major corporate financial organizations such as E. F. Hutton, which has organized a special research and promotion division to pursue these strategies.[57] In a recent hearing before the Joint Economic Committee Congress of the United States in Albany, New York, presiding member Alfonsè D'Amato proposed that the federal government provide tax incentives to private corporations to "allow the private sector more involvement in the construction of prisons, jails, and detention centers . . . [since] private corporations can build prisons for 75 percent of what it would cost state and local governments."[58]

In the area of facility management, an array of contracts with various levels of government is already in existence. At the federal level, the Immigration and Naturalization Services had nine contracts with the private sector to run detention centers for illegal aliens, while the US Marshals and the Federal Bureau of Prisons have a number of similar arrangements. Twenty-eight states reported the use of privately operated pre-release, work-release, or halfway houses, two interstate facilities for protective custody arrangements, and 1,877 privately operated residential programs for juveniles. "Much like the business of running a full-service hotel, private vendors either supply the space or take over an existing public building; room rates are established based on capital investments, operating costs, and expected occupancy; and the government is generally charged by the day for each detainee."[59] Taking the lead in this area has been Corrections Corporation of America which currently operates a "work-farm" facility in Hamilton County, Tennessee. To date, private operations have been limited to specialized populations rather than typical state penitentiary inmates. However, the Kentucky Corrections Cabinet has announced plans to contract for the housing of 200 sentenced felons.

In the area of juvenile corrections, the use of private facilities has existed for some time, yet few government agencies or social scientists have paid them much attention. In 1974, the Law Enforcement Assistance Administration (LEAA) began including private correctional facilities in its *Children in Custody* (CIC) survey conducted by the US Bureau of the Census. This census, and those that have followed, reveal both the considerable degree of private sector involvement in juvenile corrections, and the fact that such involvement has accelerated in response to the decarceration movement in public facilities.[60] A private facility is defined as being subject to government licensing, but "under the direct administrative and operational control of private enterprise, [and] typically receives substantial governmental funding, in addition to support by private sources." In order to be included in the CIC survey, at least ten percent of the facilities' population had to have been adjudicated as delinquent, declared in need of supervision, voluntarily committed and/or pending disposition by court.

The overwhelming majority of private facilities are classified by the CIC as "long-term" institutions, mainly group homes and ranches, with "open" physical environment and daily access to the community. By contrast, those facilities under public control are divided almost evenly as long- and short-term, are mostly training schools and detention centers, and are more likely to have "institutional" environments and less likely to have frequent access to the community. These selected characteristics have not varied substantially during the decade starting from the first survey in 1974 until the latest, 1983.

In 1974, there were 1,337 private facilities with 31,749 juvenile residents, while public facilities that year numbered 829 with a census count of 44,922. By 1983, the number of private facilities had risen to 1,877 while the number of residents, measured in one-day counts, after dropping slightly, returned to 31,473. The number of public institutions also increased during the period to 1,023 and the resident census rose to 50,799. Yet, by using admissions data, a somewhat different measure of facility utilization provided by the CIC survey, Barry Krisberg and Ira Schwartz point out that while these data indicate a modest decrease (−11 percent in rates per 100,000) in the overall use of public sector facilities, there has been a significant decrease in female use (−37.5 percent). Moreover, the authors note that there has been a corresponding *increase* in private sector admissions, stating that there were

> 42,005 admissions to private facilities in 1974 compared with 49,298 admissions in 1979 – an increase of 17.4 percent in total admissions. The rate of male private admissions changed by only 13.0 percent between 1974–1979 compared to a significant increase of 36.0 percent for females suggesting that females have been transferred from the public correctional system to privately operated facilities.[61]

What these and other data indicate is that the private sector has moved in as public responsibility for formal social control has been withdrawn, facilitating both transinstitutionalization, rather than actual decarceration, and "privatization." In Massachusetts for example, site of the most radical withdrawal of state authority in 1972, the situation was characterized this way:

> No alternative placements were available for most of the youth suddenly decarcerated, and makeshift settings had to be rapidly created. Private providers responded quickly; contracts were signed and Massachusetts' purchase-of-services system began its rapid expansion . . . The rapidity of this conversion for the state as a whole is shown by the rise in Massachusetts' spending for privately purchased human services in all categories, from $25 million in fiscal

1969 to $300 million in fiscal 1981. More specifically, by 1975 the total number of residential programs for court-involved youth had climbed from 9 to 95, 93 percent of which were privately run.[62]

To date, the financial status of most private juvenile correctional facilities remains somewhat of a mystery (the CIC survey does not inquire as to whether the facilities are non-profit or not). However, the important distinction here is that they are not under direct public sector control, even though they may be supported almost entirely by the state. And while the typical private facility is a small group home with about 15 residents, economic incentives, even for non-profit organizations, are in the direction of expansion. Again, the Massachusetts case points to this almost inevitable trend:

> When the purchase-of-services system first began providing services to youth in Massachusetts, the system was characterized by small, independent, low-budget operations that provided community based programs. This is no longer the case, however. DARE, Inc., for example, which opened the first group home for adolescents in Massachusetts at the beginning of the 1970s, now provides services to court-involved youth through 12 separate programs across the state. In addition, this conglomerate has branched out into services to the mentally retarded and even to adult mental health populations, and now contracts with four different [social service] agencies. The Massachusetts Taxpayers Foundation (1980) estimated that these contracts totaled $3 million dollars annually by 1979.[63]

Given recent developments in adult corrections by for-profit corporations and financial institutions, it would not be unexpected for these organizations to become heavily involved in juvenile corrections as well.

Adolescents Go from Bad to Mad

In addition to the expansion of private sector involvement in juvenile corrections, the withdrawal of direct responsibility by the state for certain classifications of misbehaving youth has resulted in an increase in the use of medicalized facilities to treat adolescents. This system of social control has developed in response not only to public sector decarceration but also to a more pervasive and long-term process of the medicalization of deviance. During the last 100 years or so, behaviors which were once seen as instances of immorality or evil – including delinquency – have been reinterpreted as symptoms of sickness or disease.[64] Furthermore, increasing numbers and types of deviant behaviors have been treated in those institutions designed for the ill – hospitals and clinics – and with the sorts of psychological and somatic therapies deemed suitable to those who are seen as in trouble, rather than as causing trouble.

A number of factors have fostered this movement in the treatment of adolescent misbehavior. One was the sequence of legislation that mandated coverage of psychiatric treatment, particularly inpatient treatment, by both public insurance providers such as Medicare and by private providers such as Blue Cross and Blue Shield. Insurance coverage made mental hospitals accessible to many non-indigent individuals who would otherwise not have been able to utilize inpatient psychiatric services either for themselves or for their offspring. Secondly, as I have shown above, public sector deinstitutionalization had a particular effect upon juveniles, primarily status offenders. These federal and state level initiatives diverted juvenile status offenders from the public justice system. Yet, just because the state decriminalized juvenile behaviors such as running away, does not mean that kids are no longer running away. As we saw in the Massachusetts case, few alternatives were available to public social control agents and parents to control their seemingly out of control adolescents. Here again, the private sector has stepped in to fill the gap left by the state.

The federal decarceration policies outlined above encouraged the states, using fiscal incentives, to deinstitutionalize status offenders from public correctional facilities. As earlier work on this movement indicates, this left the states still able to utilize private correctional as well as public and private mental health inpatient facilities for "deinstitutionalized" juveniles.[65] This private mental health sector has been characterized by some as a "hidden system" of adolescent social control, because many facilities are not subject to public scrutiny via due process procedures and because until recently, private sector institutions have been overlooked by social scientist and investigators assessing juvenile care and control.[66] This "hidden system" involves at least the following types of residential facility for juveniles: private psychiatric hospitals or wings of general hospitals for those under 18, residential treatment centers (RTCs), and, most recently, chemical dependency inpatient facilities (CDUs).

In the case of psychiatric hospitalization, gatekeepers to both public and private mental hospitals, and the insurance providers, require a diagnosis of psychiatric disorder taken from the Diagnostic and Statistical Manual (DSM III) of the American Psychiatric Association.[67] While on the face of it, this diagnostic requirement would hamper the admission of non-schizophrenic or non-psychotic youth to psychiatric hospitals, in fact there are a number of diagnoses which can fit wayward or delinquent youth. For example, the DSM III category Conduct Disorder is defined as a

> repetitive and persistent pattern of aggressive conduct by either physical violence against persons, or thefts outside the home involving confrontation with a victim. . . . The nonaggressive types are characterized by the absence of physical violence . . . However, there is a persistent pattern of conduct in conflict with norms for their age, which may take the form of. . . . persistent truancy and substance abuse; running away from home over night . . . persistent serious lying . . . vandalism or fire setting; or stealing.[68]

National data indicate the increasing use of private psychiatric hospitalization as a means of controlling misbehaving youth, while national and local data specify some of the dimensions of this increasing privatization. National data show that juvenile inpatient hospitalization more than doubled between 1970 and 1975, with an increase from 6,425 to 15,462. The increase leveled off between 1975 and 1980 rising to 16,735 inpatients. Overall these changes represent a 159 percent increase for the decade.[69] The rates of private psychiatric hospitalization for all age groups show an increase from 1970, which is interesting in the light of deinstitutionalization policy and the decline in the state hospital population. For the general population, the rate per 100,000 was 43.3 in 1970, rising to 62.6 in 1980. The rate of increase for the under-18 population was even more dramatic. In 1970 it was 9.3, in 1975 23.3, and by 1980 it was 26.3 – more than doubling in a decade. In a 1983 membership survey, the National Association of Private Psychiatric Hospitals (NAPPH) found that of the 140 hospitals responding to the age census question, the average daily census per hospital was 14.6 children and 31.7 adolescents. Average yearly per-hospital admissions were 54.1 children and 136.9 adolescents. Thus the yearly total for NAPPH membership for hospitalized juveniles under 18 in 1983 exceeded 26,740. Officials of NAPPH projected a fourfold increase in juvenile psychiatric hospitalization rates between 1980 and 1985, although they were unable to provide specific data for years otner than 1983.[70]

A California study of four juvenile psychiatric hospitals in Los Angeles from 1976 to 1979 provides a comparison between a public facility and three different private facilities.[71] The study found that the private mental health system (at least for this location during the late 1970s) tended to be less minority-oriented as well as less predominantly male than the juvenile justice system, and included middle- as well as lower-class SES youngsters. The California study also indicated that, in a system which permits privatized health care, less psychiatric care is provided where there is more need and more care where there is less need. Of the four psychiatric hospitals or wings studied, the public hospital sample experienced shorter stays and higher levels of pathology, while the private hospitals demonstrated the reverse relationship: longer stays and lower levels of pathology. The mean stay in the county hospital was 13 days; the private hospital means ranged from 25 to 106 days. The schizophrenic or psychotic diagnosis rate was 29.5 percent in the public hospital, and ranged from 12.4 to 19.5 percent in the private hospitals. The private hospital clientele was made up primarily of juveniles with DSM II antisocial, personality disorder, depressive, drug abuse or runaway reaction types of diagnosis.[72]

Data from Minnesota indicate the significant contribution of insurance coverage to the increase and expansion of adolescent psychiatric commitment. The cost of treatment in these institutions is very high, ranging from $200 to over $1,000 per patient per day, a cost borne primarily by private insurance carriers. Insurance data from Minneapolis indicate that in 1976 there were 1,123 admissions of adolescents to private psychiatric hospitals in the local area which were reimbursed by either Blue Cross or Blue Shield, accounting for 46,718 patient days, while in only the first six months of 1983 the figures were 1,124 and 43,855 respectively. The rate per 100,000 population was 187 in 1976 and by 1983 it had risen to 412.[73]

The data for all private psychiatric hospitals also indicate the typical ownership patterns for this type of institution, and thus of the specific forms of privatization. Of the 184 private hospitals in the United States in January 1980, 63 (42 percent of available beds) were non-profit, while 121 (with 58 percent of the beds), were for-profit. Among the for-profit hospitals, the majority were owned by corporations (109), seven were owned by individuals and five by partnerships.[74] In the 1983 NAPPH survey cited above, 68 of the responding facilities (46 percent) were multi-facility and for-profit, 28 (19 percent) were independent and for-profit, while 51 (35 percent) were not-for-profit. These figures represent an increase in privatization and profitization over time. As NIMH analysts Thompson, Bass and Witkin (1982) note:

Between 1968 and 1975 the number of for-profit psychiatric

hospitals run by corporations grew from 62 to 103 (an increase of 66 percent) while for-profit private psychiatric hospitals owned by individuals or partnerships decreased from 20 to 14, a drop of 30 percent. Not-for-profit, church-related private psychiatric hospitals decreased from 17 to 8, a 53 percent decline and not-for-profit hospitals increased only slightly, from 52 to 55, or by 6 percent.[75]

Like nursing homes (see above) and American medicine in general, inpatient psychiatric medicine is becoming increasingly dominated by the corporate sector. While private psychiatric hospitals have always been a part of the American health scene, they were, prior to the mid-1970s, primarily owner-operated organizations, run by small groups of practicing psychiatrists. Today, the private psychiatric sector is dominated by large corporate, investor-owned, for-profit, multi-hospital chains of which there were 30 by 1984. While the majority were general hospital operations, nearly half also operated freestanding psychiatric facilities. The largest 20 firms had combined revenues of $11 billion and combined profits of $700 million in 1983 – up 38 percent since 1982.[76]

In order to get a sense of the size and scope of some of these organizations, the description of selected characteristics of particular firms is in order. The largest multi-hospital organization is Hospital Corporation of America which, in 1983, posted revenues of $3.2 billion, $4 billion in assest and had 71,000 employees in facilities in 41 states and five foreign countries according to Standard and Poor's business directory. The firm controlled 3,200 psychiatric beds in 25 freestanding facilities. Other firms include American Medical International which established a corporate division for psychiatric facilities in 1983, National Medical Enterprises which entered in 1982 through a corporate merger with Psychiatric Institutes of America, and finally, Comprehensive Care Corporation which operates primarily as a contract manager for psychiatric and substance abuse treatment programs in general hospitals.[77] One of CompCare's specialties is adolescent psychiatry.

Thus, today one segment of the medicalized private sector of juveniles is the psychiatric hospital, often profit-making and owned by a corporation, which provides care and control of misbehaving or disturbed adolescents (and sometimes children) in return for insurance money. Variations on this system include psychiatric wings of private general hospitals, which may be even more profitable and widespread.[78] Psychiatric facilities are used both by the public juvenile welfare and justice system – as a placement alternative for disturbed wards of the court – and by parents as a relief from hostile or uncontrollable youth. Some of the patients in juvenile psychiatric institutions are severely mentally disturbed, manifesting the delusions and hallucinations characteristic of schizophrenia of psychoses; the typical adolescent tends to enter treatment with a conduct or personality disorder diagnosis.

In addition to psychiatric hospitalization, other mental health-related institutions have also come to serve the function of care and control of misbehaving youth. Among them are institutions which have existed for some time, such as residential treatment centers (RTCs), and those which are of more recent development, such as chemical dependency units (CDUs) of general or psychiatric hospitals. The purpose of RTCs is the "provision of round-the-clock care to persons primarily under the age of 18 who are diagnosed as having an emotional or mental disorder."[79] Over 95 percent of RTCs in 1979 were private. The 1979 admission rate to RTCs nationwide – 15,453, or 24 per 100,000 – was almost the same as the 1980 rate for juvenile psychiatric inpatients. Adding together RTC and private psychiatric hospitals' yearly census, we find that there were well over 30,000 juveniles under 18 in private mental health facilities at the beginning of the 1980s.

While there were only 184 private psychiatric hospitals (for all ages) in the United States, in 1980, there were 368 RTCs. In 1979 statistics represent an increase in admissions to RTCs since the early 1970s, although not as dramatic as that in the private psychiatric hospital sector; in 1980 there were 29 percent more admissions to RTCs than in 1971.[80] Despite their similarities to private psychiatric facilities, the RTCs are different with respect to cost. While private psychiatric hospital fees may exceed $1,000 a day, their average expenditures per resident per day in 1979 was $153, according to NIMH.[81] RTCs on the other hand, had a daily per patient expenditure of $69 in 1983. Despite their private ownership, most of the referrals to RTCs come from the public sector, through social welfare agencies responding to complaints from the child's school, placement, or home.[82]

Another more recent institutional form for adolescent care and control is the chemical dependency unit, on which, given that it is a relatively new phenomenon, available data are scarce. Barry Krisberg and Ira Schwartz, in discussing this aspect of the private medical system in Minneapolis, state that, "In 1980, there were an estimated 3,000 to 4,000 juveniles admitted to inpatient chemical dependency treatment programs. Although it is unknown how many juveniles were admitted to such programs in the early 1970s, it is assumed that the numbers were substantially less because there were few chemical dependency centers at that time."[83] Evidence from the 1983 NAPPH survey indicates a high incidence of drug and alcohol dependency treatment within the private psychiatric sector on a nationwide basis. Unfortunately, these data show neither trends over time, nor specification by age. But in 1983 the NAPPH member hospitals reported an average of 234.6 dependency admissions for each of the 147 responding hospitals, with an average daily census of 17.9.[84]

Comprehensive Care Corporation cited above is a leader in the business of treating both adult and adolescent substance abusers. The company advertises heavily in many urban markets, prompting parents to commit their children "before something serious happens" (i.e., they are arrested and possibly drawn into the public correctional system). Through the use of its contract system, the company runs over 100 hospitals in addition to its own ten freestanding units which had revenues of $73 million in 1982 and profits of $7.6 million according to the company portfolio. The company is considered, in investment terminology, a "pure play" in the for-profit health care system. In summary, these data suggest that in addition to a burgeoning private correctional system, significant numbers of young people are being treated in a privatized, for-profit medical care and control system in the current post-public, decarceration period.

What do these developments in the evolution of the social control sub-apparatus signal? Does the apparant shifting of responsibility from public to "private" auspices represent a significant change in the nature of the American welfare state? Has the state divested itself and *de*structed its care and control apparatus, or has it instead, incorporated new institutional forms under the rubric of the state? Important implications of these questions are considered in the final chapter.

7

The Evolution of the State Apparatus

"[A] democratic government increases its power simply by the fact of its permanence," stated Alexis de Tocqueville, reflecting on developments in the United States. "Time is on its side; every incident befriends it; the passions of individuals unconsciously promote it; and may be asserted, that the older a democratic community is, the more centralized will its government become..."[1] While our nineteenth-century observer could not have possibly imagined our present-day world, his prophecy looms heavily over our assessment of nearly 200 years of American state building. From the establishment of truly bureaucratic state governments at the turn of the century through the explosion of federal bureaucratic goods and services during the 1960s, we have seen the increasing centralization as well as expansion of the US state apparatus. I have shown this movement to be the result of the intersection of three forms of social action: the crisis management role of the capitalist state; the activities of state managers and political parties as they attempt to use the state apparatus to further their own interests; and the unintended consequences of state policies.

In the preceding pages I have explored the changing practices of how we, as a society, have responded to matters of deviance, illness, crime, and poverty. We have seen how, not unlike other modern societies, it is the state that has taken on the primary role in addressing problems of social control in America. Thus my approach has been state-centered, highlighting the role of the state as an administrative, legal, bureaucratic, and coercive organization possessing a unique form of power. Rather than revealing a steady movement from cruelty to enlightenment, my historical survey of social control presents a far more ambiguous picture. Indeed, in reviewing this period of history, one is struck by the fluctuating, cyclical, and often contradictory nature of state policies. I have attempted to link the failures and limitations of these policies not to the need for "better planning and administration," but rather to the self-obstructive nature of the policy-making capacity of the state itself.

My narrative began by examining America's first primary institutions of social control – the prison and the poorhouse. I argued that the proliferation of these institutions was engendered, in part, by the rise of Accumulative State which had the effect of accelerating the breakdown of community cohesiveness and isolation and hence the practicality and effectiveness of non-institutional social control. Once established, however, the nineteenth-century penitentiary dramatized the tension between the public demand for the incarceration and punishment of criminals, and the administrative and fiscal burden of providing such arrangements. Here state managers were able to balance these imperatives, at least for a time, through the sale of inmate labor power in a cooperative venture with private capital. This extension of state power ultimately failed as public policy, however, caught in the shifting nexus of state/society relations. The poor or almshouse, on the other hand, was quite simply a failure at instilling the "habits of industry" in its charges. While it never lived up to this noble mission, it did function, at least for a while, as a "last resort" for poverty and dependency, thereby ensuring a rough distinction between the "deserving" and "undeserving" poor. Yet, in time, the deteriorating conditions of these "all-purpose" institutions became a rallying point for religious and social reformers, and threatened to expose state managers as cruel and neglectful.

With the rise of an urban and industrial society in the late nineteenth century we saw a corresponding change in the form of the state, the functions it prioritized, and the apparatus through which it exercised its power. The Bureaucratic State

produced segregative modes of care and control: specialized
institutions which classified the troublesome populations. The
almshouse gave way to new facilities in which the able-bodied
poor were separated from the helpless, the insane from the
criminal and the vagabond from the indigent and aged. A
reformist ideology suggested that these institutions would be
more effective at classifying, curing and correcting recalcitrant
citizens. But these organizations created the need for a centralized administration which served to expand the reach of the
state apparatus and consolidate political power in regional
government.

The crisis of the depression and the war changed much of
this. These emergencies shifted responsibility *and* political
power to a rapidly expanding national administration. In
response to the economic contraction of the late 1920s, massive
government spending through the transfer of federal funds to
state governments reproduced the existing state level social
control sub-apparatus. By this time, legal and ethical issues had
challenged the legitimacy of the contracting out of inmate
labor, while unions and manufacturers resisted the selling of
institutionally created products. Moreover, the self-
reproducing labor of inmates inside institutions could not offset
the rising service and maintenance costs of these non-market,
public sector facilities. Thus, by mid-twentieth century, we saw
the accumulation of thousands and thousands of people in
America's extensive care and control apparatus.

The post-war period brought profound change to the institutional structure of American capitalism, and with it, a new
American state. Political battles over the course of the new
Liberal Welfare State were fought between conservative political parties and bureaucratic interests, ultimately placing great
strains on local and regional government in the 1950s. It is here
that we saw the first evidence of a turning away from traditional
public institutions as the organizational legitimacy of the state
hospital was attacked and the initial evidence of "deinstitutionalization" appeared. But it was in the 1960s that the practice took
hold. Fusing fiscal conservatism with powerful ideological
movements critical of the "total institution" and advocating the
rights of patients and prisoners, decarceration was a poli-

which suited all political agendas.[2] It was particularly suited, I have argued, to the Kennedy administration, where community-based social policies were woven into a plan to enhance political power and complement the regime's macroeconomic goals. Yet by the lat 1960s, the post-war New Deal coalition was in shambles and the economic climate was characterized by "stagflation." The decarceration movement was accelerated in these years when the conservative administrations of Nixon and Ford were confronted by the "fiscal crisis" of the 1970s. Thus, as I have argued, the practical application of the latest reform movement was the creation of a care and control void, increasingly filled with both neglect and marginalization, as well as a tendency toward new forms of institutional care and control.

The Dialectics of the State in Civil Society

I began this book by asserting that the historical study of social control could be advanced by taking a state-centered viewpoint. Standing this declaration on its head, I now want to pose the question, what has my examination of American social control practice told us about the development of the American welfare state form? Like the ideal-typical "liberal welfare model" suggested by Marie Ruggie, the evolution of the American state reflects a pattern of incremental, ad hoc, intervention and institution-building, and thus the creation of a fragmented and weakly integrated apparatus. She states that:

> The ability of such a system to synoptic conception of problems is limited. Since the fundamental position of the market structuring social relations is maintained, market created social problems are forever reproduced. Ironically, while the intent of the liberal welfare state is to play as minimal a role as possible in intervening in the affairs of society, the structural reproduction of social problems necessitates a constant and ever-increasing state presence [3]

Put another way, the crisis management function of the liberal welfare state necessitates the increasing exercise of its infrastructural power.

The expansion of such power in the United States in the post-war period had been countered by the rise of powerful professional and socioeconomic groups whose interests lie in shaping the policies and practices of the state apparatus. Given its commitment to market-based social relations, the American liberal welfare state has – particularly during times of heightened fiscal and political conflict – relied on such groups to perform its functions. We have thus seen the expansion of para-apparatus agencies and institutions and the progressive infusion of interests across the state/society nexus. Unlike true corporatist structures where organized producer groups are systematically integrated into the decisional structure of the state through a system of representation and mutual cooperation, the liberal welfare state proceeds more haphazardly. Here no real organizational or decisional integration takes place, contributing to what John Keane calls, "clumsy and fluctuating patterns of intervention, withdrawal and compromise,"[4] Do these "quasi-corporatist" structures and the patterns Keane characterizes represent a significant change in the nature of the American state? In some ways, no. We saw a similar process take place concerning prison labor in the nineteenth century. What has changed in the contemporary period is the intensity and pervasiveness of the formation.

What are the effects of these developments on the ability of the liberal welfare state to plan rational public policy? With the infusion of special interests into the state apparatus, policy implementation and outcome is shaped within a matrix of power/conflict rather than balanced public interest. The various sub-apparatus of the state thus become an arena of class/group conflict distorting policy goals and generating "planning failures." The response to such failures may be a reordering of priorities or the creation of a new sub-apparatus. Yet since interests, both in and out of the state, may be embedded in the obsolete organization, it must often exist alongside the new, creating conflict over resources, jurisdiction, and power. For instance, despite the policy shift away from the state mental hospital in the 1960s, many of these institutions still exist today – half emptied and as costly as ever – operating in the same system as community mental health facilities. The interests of state employee unions, professional groups, and the communities in which they are located have ensured their survival.

These problems are only heightened with the expansion of those para-apparatus agencies and institutions who lie outside the sphere of direct state control. Here the typical struggle for coordination between state bureaucracies is exacerbated by the addition of "outside" organizations which may or may not be integrated into policy objectives or be fully accountable to the state and the public. State managers are left with the task of trying to impart order and rationality over a heterogeneous collection of institutions and agencies with a variety of organizational, legal, economic, and political ties to the state.

In assessing the deinstitutionalization policies of 1960s and 1970s, much of the "revisionist" writing of the last few years has suggested that these actions reflected the state's attempt to divest itself of the administrative and fiscal burden of welfare state services.[5] Yet, despite the proliferation of privately-run care and control organizations, has this meant that the state has really divested itself or, is it that the state has actually reconstituted its power, incorporating new institutional forms under its own rubric? In a recent essay, John Lowman, Robert Menzies, and T. S. Palys argue that to draw a rigid distinction between "private" and "public" modes of social control is "theoretically fruitless," given the inter-relationship between the state and civil society. The authors argue that such a differentiation "ignores the probability that the 'private' agents of control are either directly or indirectly supported by the public sector," and contend that the interesting questions concern the dialectical relationship between these sectors.[6] Thus, Lowman et al. see the newly "privatized" and decentralized system as an extension rather than a reduction in state power and control. While I am in basic agreement with these authors, a few points need to be made.

The first is that, historically, in the US the state's attempt to respond to various "social problems" has often resulted in expanding the power and domain of the state rather than "solving" these problems. This seems clear from my own analysis. Yet while the penetration of the state into everyday life may appear to be both historically linear and one-sided – that is, state-derived – its development is, in fact, reflective of a more fluid and dynamic relationship in social development. This suggests that the relationship between the state and civil society is, indeed, dialectical, one influencing and shaping the development of the other across an ill-defined threshold. Social practices and techniques originating in civil society may be adopted by the state and vice-versa.[7] The challenge for the social analyst is to identify those historical junctures where significant changes occur and to understand their causes and consequences. The emergence of new forms of privatized care and control institutions is a case in point.

These organizations represent and are constituted by *both* the state and civil society simultaneously – each divesting while investing, decentralizing while centralizing, and displacing power while concentrating it. On the one hand, there are private psychiatric hospitals for misbehaving youth that exist entirely outside the fiscal and administrative umbrella of the state. State policies, however, created the conditions for their genesis and continue to permit their existence. For now, a portion of the care and control function of the society is located within the sphere of civil society. On the other hand, we have "private" board and care homes which provide living arrangements for indigent clientele in exchange for reimbursement by the state. Here the practical linkages to the state are more direct, rendering these "private" organizations part of the para-apparatus of the state and therefore its power and authority.

Finally, despite this constant adjustment and creation of new organizational forms, there remain distinct differences, both in theory and practice, between more privatized modes of care and their public sector counterparts. It would be unwise to neglect these differences and to over-emphasize their relationship to state power and apparatus. Despite the permeation of the state into everyday life, there is still a separation (albeit flexible), between the state and the economic and social/cultural spheres of society in contemporary America. A fundamental condition of the state in this society is that it is excluded from organizing and governing "private" economic relations and cultural, legal, and philosophical mechanisms ensure that this is the case. Capitalism is alive and well and Beverly Enterprises or Comprehensive Care, Inc. are not "the state." They exist to make or lose a profit, merge with other companies, or simply go out of business.

The use of these kinds of privatized care and control institutions shifts the organizational structurating principles (i.e. the practices that produce and reproduce these associated forms within the *duree* of daily life) from non-market to market based. This alteration has critical implications for the state and public policy. On the one hand, attempts by state managers to privatize these functions may check the expansion of the state apparatus and the tendency for state run, non-market organizations to consume increasing amounts of resources. On the other hand, the development of market based organization encourages private accumulation and investment, increases the material basis of the state through tax collection, and thus aids in state reproduction. Moreover, by privatizing social control activities, the state no longer wholly subsidizes the "market value" of institutionalized inmates; these individuals themselves have become commodities. In this new form, their "value" exists within the state's ability to exchange capital for their care and control.[8]

Yet not unlike past actions by state managers, this privatizing strategy is fraught with contradictions, and challenges the very basis on which the state was called upon to intervene in the first place. When the state incarcerates a criminal in a public facility, for example, the ultimate goal of this incarceration is the reintegration of him/her into civil society. Thus, a primary structuring principle of a non-market, public institution is the practice of transforming, through care and/or control, "troublesome" individuals into citizens who engage in some form of private commodity exchange.

By contrast, the very act of incarceration in a private facility creates a commodified form. The transformation process – a basic rationale of the practice of public facilities – becomes secondary. Rather, the primary structurating principle of this organization is the accumulation of capital through market exchange. Even a rudimentary understanding of the logic of capital accumulation tells us that this fundamental objective runs counter to the political, as well as the societal goal of the provision of transformative care and control. Thus, once the practice of care and control (or for that matter, mass transit, utilities, and the like) is shifted to private accumulation units, then "social policy" (both political power and the "public good") is subordinated to private decision making.[9] For example, the state may arrange an elaborate scheme involving the private sector, only to find that the organization has deemed some other market for goods or services more profitable, and has simply gone out of the care and control business.

Thus the state, in order to retain the services of its "partner," has to ensure that adequate profits are to be had. Yet, in a care and control market place where there is competition for available funds, the incentive for the private organization is to cut costs, which may ultimately result in a reduction in the "quality of life" of its clients. Faced with a potential legitimation crisis, state managers must then regulate and control these private organizations which may in turn, have the effect of reducing profits. In a privatized care and control system where the state provides financial reimbursement, the state is subsidizing private profit. Thus, the incentive of the privatized organization lies not in the transformative process but rather in the creation and preservation of a market of "troublesome" individuals and the absorption of as much state subsidized profit as possible. In short, while the privatization of the state's care and control practice may have been in the immediate interest of the state at a certain historical juncture, it may leave state managers constantly confronted by potential crises of private accumulation on the one hand, and threats to their own legitimacy on the other. Ultimately, how state managers confront this position will depend upon their negotiation of the shifting boundary between the state and civil society.

Appendix: Concepts, Data, and Sources

I would like to begin by setting out some conceptual boundaries. If there was ever a term ubiquitous yet thoroughly misused in the social sciences it is "social control." It has, indeed become, as Stanley Cohen put it, a "Mickey Mouse" concept.[1] For lack of a better alternative, however, Cohen, myself and others continue to employ it. For purposes of this analysis, the concept of "social control" refers narrowly to those practices, from imprisonment to mental hospitalization, by which "troublesome" populations are removed from the everyday life of society. I sometimes use the terms "care and control" because, quite obviously, some practices involve the provision of medical, personal, or social care, while others are principally concerned with physical confinement. Still others combine both functions. Yet even when "care" is involved, many institutions use the legal power of the state to force an individual to submit to such care.

Nanette Davis and Bo Anderson have described a number of "ideal-types" of control organizations based on the dimensions of (1) the mode or source of control and (2) the degree of pervasiveness in the organization.[2] "Internalized" control is by normative consensus while "externalized" control is based on a hierarchical relationship implying social distance between the controller and the controlled. Pervasiveness refers to the degree to which the organization regulates the day-to-day activities of its clients. In this study I deal primarily with institutions high in pervasiveness and with external modes of control – essentially what Erving Goffman called "total institutions."[3]

The institutions I have chosen to include in my analysis reflect their relative importance in a given historical context. By "importance," I am referring to the degree to which these facilities are relied upon to provide care and control services. Universal examples include adult prisons, juvenile correctional facilities, and mental hospitals, while historically specific institutions include the poor or almshouse, the psychopathic hospital, and the board and care home. By focusing on institutional forms of social control I am not suggesting that these are the only, or necessarily the most important forms of control in American society. Nor do I assume that the state has a monopoly on the social control "market" of the society. These institutions are simply one response, one expression of coercive power.

The existence of such power implies a dichotomy between the controlled and the controllers. This relationship manifests itself quite clearly in the wards of the state hospital and in the prison yards. But the process through which the coercive power of the state is evoked, filling those wards and yards with individuals, is far less conspicuous. By using the term "social control" I do not wish to imply, like many "revisionists," that the asylum or the prison were instruments of power used by one class (in society *or* the state) against another. This view imparts a passivity to, say, the working class, which seems wholly unwarranted. An angry spouse, a fellow worker, or an exasperated parent may initiate the power of the state in a way not unlike the actions of a propertied class against those not bound by property.

In the course of my analysis, I have chosen a variety of sources, including primary materials such as published governmental data, professional journals, presidential papers, texts of speeches, the proceedings of meetings of relevant organizations, the congressional record, and the like. Principal examples include: the US Bureau of the Census special reports on institutional populations, *Historical Statistics of the United States: Colonial Times to 1970*, and the *Statistical Abstract of the United States*; the *American Journal of Psychiatry* the annual proceedings of the National Prison Association, the American Correctional Association, the American Psychiatric Association, and the archives of the Council on State Governments. In order to "fill in the gaps" where primary sources were either not readily available (or where to survey them would be impractical given the span of history I proposed to cover), I rely on secondary sources, mainly reputable historical narratives that provide a chronological account of documented "factual events." Examples of secondary materials include: David Rothman's extensively researched, *The Discovery of the Asylum*, as well as his *Conscience and Convenience*; *The History of Public Welfare in New York State, 1867–1940* by David Schneider and Albert Deutsch; Blake McKelvey's *American Prisons*; and *The Evolution of Penology in Pennsylvania* (1927) by Harry Elmer Barnes. When relying on secondary materials, I have, whenever possible, attempted to verify either those primary sources cited or cross-checked these secondary works with others in order to corroborate the generally accepted historical literature.

My selection principles for the inclusion of both primary and secondary data were as follows: (1) that the data and source had a reasonable degree of both reliability and face validity concerning the question at hand. (2) That the data reflected a certain degree of representativeness. In general, I assess and document national trends, although I do use state-wide data, often more detailed, in order to further illustrate and highlight national changes. Moreover, I have provided, wherever possible, standardized rates in order to account for population shifts. And (3), while I have of course marshalled as much evidence as I can in support of my arguments, this was never to the known or systematic exclusion of opposing data. Since in the end, the success or failure of my thesis lies in my ability to convince the reader that both the trends that I have documented and the interpretations I draw from this evidence are valid, then this alone remains the ultimate test of the appropriateness of the data I have chosen.

As the reader will observe, much of the data cited throughout this study is from primary, publicly available, government published sources. As social scientists, we are intimately familiar with such sources of data, so much so that, to many, these "social facts" have become unquestionable in their accuracy and representation. I assume, however, that these data are fairly crude measures of the particular variable in question. Clearly, the reliability of data such as the population census has increased over time, and when one is seeking information about a period of time a century ago, one has to approach these figures cautiously. Often, however, official data are all that is available, and under these circumstances, I have tried to indicate in the text or in endnotes where reliability and/or validity is particularly in question.

Other factors further complicate the use of official types of data. The first, and most obvious, is that the data are collected more for administrative purposes rather than for social science research. Given that I have not attempted to convert such data in ways to make them more readily available for elaborate statistical analyses, this is less of a problem here. Secondly, and of particular concern when assessing trends over time, changes in methods of data collection, definitions of variables, variations in sample sizes and the like, can often make comparability across a historical period questionable. With this fact in mind, I have attempted to be as internally consistent as possible when demonstrating changes over time. That is, I try to cite data that have been collected by the same agency, using basically the same methods. Where this has not been possible, or where significant changes in the collection procedures have occurred, I have indicated as much.

Finally, a number of authors, analyzing patterns of institutionalization for a variety of populations, have themselves cited many of these same government statistics. I will sometimes reference their work in addition to or instead of the primary sources. This is the case because either (1) the primary data were unavailable to me; or (2) they reclassified, recalculated, or otherwise manipulated the data to demonstrate various relationships that are important; or (3) in order to underscore my own interpretation of the trends present in the data, I have added their assessment in an effort to provide further verification.

Notes

Chapter 1 Explaining Patterns of Institutional Social Control

1 See for example Blake McKelvey, *American Prisons: A History of Good Intentions* ([1936] 1977); David Schneider and Albert Deutsch, *The History of Public Welfare in New York State, 1867–1940* (1941); G. Zilboorg and G. Henry *A History of Medical Psychology* (1973).

2 Stanley Cohen and Andrew Scull, *Social Control and the State* (1983), p. 2.

3 See for example Dario Melossi and Massimo Parvarini, *The Prison and the Factory: Origins of the Penitentiary System*, tr. G. Cousin (1978); Anthony Platt, *The Child Savers* (1969); and Michael Ignatieff, *A Just Measure of Pain: The Penitentiary in the Industrial Revolution, 1750–1850* (1978).

4 Andrew Scull, *Decarceration: Community Treatment and the Deviant – A Radical View* ([1977] 1984); Michel Foucault, *Discipline and Punish* tr. A. M. Sheridan (1977).

5 David Rothman, *The Discovery of the Asylum: Social Order and Disorder in the New Republic* (1971).

6 See Appendix for a more extended discussion of the concept "social control."

7 John Lowman, Robert Menzies, and T. S. Palys, "Introduction: transcarceration and the modern state of penality," in *Transcarceration: Essays in the Sociology of Social Control*, eds J. Lowman, R. Menzies, and T. Palys (1987), pp. 1–26, esp. p. 5.

8 Michael Mann argues within a state-centered model that the state *is* an arena and that this is precisely the basis of its autonomy. Society-centered perspectives rarely acknowledge such auton-

omy. See "The autonomous power of the state: its origins, mechanisms and results," *Archives européennes de sociologie* (1984) pp. 185–213.

9   Much of the debate was sparked by Theda Skocpol's pathbreaking, *States and Social Revolutions: A Comparative Analysis of France, Russia, and China* (1979).

10   While I may be accused of writing "a history from the top down" by focusing on the agency of state managers, I believe that their crucial role in the structuration of these organizations warrants my state-centered viewpoint and by no means denies the contributing role of other social actors. See Appendix.

11   Michael Mann, "The autonomous power of the state."

12   I have no intention of offering a new "theory of the state" in this essay. In their book, *State Apparatus: Structures and Language of Legitimacy* (1984), Gordon Clark and Michael Dear provide an excellent review of the analytical alternatives within this highly diverse yet often overlapping literature. Elements of many of these views are contained in the form-function-apparatus framework they set out and that I adopt here. Employing this framework, as well as notions drawn from structuration theory, does not imply rigid, *a priori* theorizing. Rather, these concepts were used to "sensitize" my investigation and analysis. For the most recent statement on structuration theory see Anthony Giddens, *The Constitution of Society* (1984).

13   See Jurgen Habermas, *Legitimation Crisis*, tr. T. McCarthy (1973).

14   Clark and Dear, *State Apparatus*, pp. 48–9.

15   Such "crisis measures" are not necessarily rescinded or withdrawn completely after the precipitating event but rather may become institutionalized as more or less accepted practice.

16   While the impact of this crisis prone tendencies of capitalist development are potentially paralyzing to the society, neither Offe nor I assume any imminent "breakdown." The purpose of a critical social science is to comprehend the limits of the "policy-making capacity of the capitalist state." See Claus Offe, *Contradictions of the Welfare State*, ed. J. Keane (1984), p. 35.

17   Recent examples of state intervention in the US in response to threatening "social problems" include roadblocks to stop intoxicated drivers, the confiscating of personal property under restrictive drug laws, and proposals to regulate sexual practices in the face of Acquired Immune Deficiency Syndrome.

Chapter 2   Charting the Liberal–Capitalist State

1   Alan Wolfe, *The Limits of Legitimacy* (1977).
2   See Henry Cabot Lodge, *The Federalist: A Commentary on the Constitution of the United States* (1883); C. P. Nettles, *The Emergence of a National Economy, 1775–1815* (1964).
3   Wolfe, *The Limits of Legitimacy*, pp. 13–41.
4   See Louis Hartz, *Economic Policy and Democratic Thought: Pennsylvania, 1776–1860* (1948); Oscar Handlin and Mary Flug Handlin, *Commonwealth – A Study of the Role of Government in the American Economy: Massachusetts, 1774–1861* ([1947] 1969).
5   The fact that it is under the Accumulative State that institutional mechanisms of social control arise warrants an extended discussion of their relationship here.
6   Thomas Dumm, *Democracy and Punishment: Disciplinary Origins of the United States* (1987), p. 88.
7   Lawrence Friedman, *A History of American Law* (1973), p. 250.
8   Orlando Lewis, *The Development of American Prisons and Prison Customs, 1776–1845* ([1922] 1967), p. 18.
9   Robert Cray, *Paupers and Poor Relief in New York City and its Rural Environs, 1700–1830* (1988), p. 84.
10 Martin Shefter argues that the electoral, bureaucratic, and administrative reforms of the Jacksonian Era reflected an effort by the new majority to purge themselves of their political enemies. How this directly impacted on the "discovery of the asylum" remains at issue. See Martin Shefter, "Party, bureaucracy, and political change in the United States," in *Political Parties: Development and Decay*, eds Louis Maisel and Joseph Cooper (1978), pp. 211–66.
11 Friedman, *A History of American Law*, p. 100.
12 Christopher Lasch, *The World of Nations* (1974), p. 13.
13 As I will demonstrate in chapter 3, the complications of settlement laws and the expense of carrying out orders of removal and defending their appeals would further diminish the capacity of communities to insulate themselves and would make the "economical" almshouse that much more attractive.
14 In his *The Discovery of the Asylum: Social Order and Disorder in the New Republic* (1971), David Rothman points out, quite rightly (p. xvi), that the asylum was *not* an "automatic and inevitable response of an industrial and urban society." Yet, while this may

be true of any crude, causal argument, Rothman's preoccupation with shifting ideas and philosophies leaves little room for exploring the more subtle ways these movements shaped the responses that did appear.

15　Law enforcement as well as prison, poorhouse, and asylum administrators were all targets of the campaign against political corruption, influence and favoritism. See for example James Leiby, *Charity and Correction in New Jersey* (1967) and selected documents from different states on civil service reform in this area in Sophonisba Breckinridge, *Public Welfare Administration in the United States* (1927). See as well Martin Shefter, "Party, bureaucracy, and political change," pp. 230–7; Steven Skowronek, *Building a New American State: The Expansion of National Administrative Capacities, 1877–1920* (1982).

16　For Dario Melossi and Massimo Parvarini, for example, the "prison/factory" emerged not to produce commodities – with a goal of economic utility – but rather as a "disciplinary apparatus" with a human product to produce: "the transformation of the criminal into proletarian." The role of the state, however, goes unexamined, essentially reduced to a managerial, if not implicitly instrumental role, in the reproduction of bourgeois social order. See their *The Prison and the Factory: Origins of the Penitentiary System*, tr. G. Cousin (1978). In a similar yet broader analysis, Michel Foucault argues in *Discipline and Punish*, tr. A. M. Sheridan (1977), pp. 242–3, that the economic effect of prison labor is in "producing individuals mechanized to the general norms of an industrial society . . . [It thus constitutes] a power relation, an empty economic form, a schema of individual submission and of adjustment to a production apparatus." Given the sweeping and abstractly philosophical nature of Foucault's project however, the state remains in a shadowy and untheorized position.

17　H. C. Mohler "Convict labor policies," *Journal of Criminal Law and Criminology* (1925), pp. 557–73; E. B. Mittleman, "Prison labor in the United States," in *A History of Labor in the United States, 1895–1932*, ed. J. R. Common ([1921] 1966), pp. 327–54; David Rothman, *Conscience and Convenience: The Asylum and its Alternatives in Progressive America* (1980).

18　National Prison Association, *First Annual Report* (1884), p. 183.

19　National Prison Association, *Proceedings of the National Prison Congress* (1887), p. 217.

20　"Factory regimes" are conceived of as the political regulation of production which may be independent of the organization of production or labor process. See Michael Burawoy, "Karl Marx and the satanic mills: factory politics under early capitalism in England, United States, and Russia," *American Journal of Sociology* 90 (1984), pp. 247–82 and my own "Technology, control, and the social organization of work at a British hardware firm, 1791–1891," *American Journal of Sociology* 93 (1987), pp. 62–8.

21 US Bureau of Labor Statistics, *Convict Labor in 1923* (1925).
22 Robinson, Louis, *Should Prisoners Work?* (1931), p. 95.
23 Mohler, "Convict labor policies;" Lewis, *The Development of American Prisons*; George Ives, *A History of Penal Methods* (1914); Rothman, *The Discovery of the Asylum*.
24 From Richard Vaux, *Notices of the Original and Successive Attempts to Improve the Discipline of the Prison at Philadelphia and to Reform the Criminal Code of Pennsylvania* (1826) as quoted in Harry Barnes, *The Evolution of Penology in Pennsylvania: A Study in American Social History* (1927), pp. 87–91.
25 Barnes, *The Evolution of Penology in Pennsylvania*, p. 164.
26 Michael Hindus, *Prison and Plantation: Crime, Justice, and Authority in Massachusetts and South Carolina, 1767–1878* (1980), p. 164.
27 US Bureau of the Census, *The Historical Statistics of the United States: Colonial Times to 1957* (1960), pp. 12–14.
28 Barnes, *The Evolution of Penology in Pennsylvania*, p. 155.
29 Report of the Commissioners on the Penal Code (1828, p. 19) as quoted in Barnes, *The Evolution of Penology in Pennsylvania*, p. 155.
30 Mittleman, "Prison labor in the United States."
31 This was stated in the *Report of the Legislative Committee on Prison Discipline* of 1830 and is quoted in Harry Barnes, *A History of the Penal, Reformatory, and Correctional Institutions of the State of New Jersey* (1918), p. 84–5. Barnes reproduces the entire report in his appendix.
32 Mittleman, "Prison labor in the United States," p. 345.
33 Ibid., p. 346.
34 Barnes, *The Evolution of Penology in Pennsylvania*, p. 240.
35 Gustave de Beaumont and Alexis de Tocqueville, *On the Penitentiary System of the United States and its Application in France*, tr. Francis Lieber (1833), p. 59.
36 Inspectors of the Eastern Penitentiary (Pennsylvania), *Annual Report* (1855), pp. 8–9.

37 Inspectors of the Eastern Penitentiary (Pennsylvania), *Annual Report* (1880), p. 7.

38 Inspectors of the Eastern Penitentiary (Pennsylvania), *Annual Report* (1837), p. 5.

39 Barnes, *The Evolution of Penology in Pennsylvania*, p. 287.

40 See Note No. 31, Barnes, *A History of the Penal, Reformatory, and Correctional Institutions of the State of New Jersey*, pp. 396–425.

41 Inspectors of the Western Penitentiary (Pennsylvania), *Annual Report* (1867), p. 8.

42 See Mohler, "Convict Labor Policies;" John Commons, *History of Labor in the United States, 1895–1932* ([1921] 1966); H. B. Gill, "The prison labor problem," in *Prisons of Tomorrow*, eds. E. H. Sutherland and T. Sellin (1931), pp. 83–101.

43 Rothman, *Conscience and Convenience* (1980), p. 139; see also the Texas Penitentiary Committee, *Report of Findings* (1913).

44 Blake McKelvey, *American Prisons: A History of Good Intentions* ([1936] 1977), p. 117.

45 US Department of Labor, *Convict Labor, 1886* (1887); US Bureau of Labor Statistics, *Convict Labor in 1923*.

46 Gill, "The prison labor problem," p. 88.

47 Robinson, *Should Prisoners Work?*, pp. 235–45.

48 Hindus, *Prison and Plantation*, p. 166–7.

49 Inspectors of the Eastern Penitentiary (Pennsylvania), *Annual Reports* (1880), p. 7.

50 S. Messinger, J. E. Berecochea, D. Rauma, and R. A. Berk, "The foundations of parole in California," *Law and Society Review* 19 (1985), pp. 69–106.

51 Anthony Platt, *The Child Savers* (1969), p. 105.

52 David Schneider and Albert Deutsch, *The History of Public Welfare in New York State, 1867–1940* (1941), p. 84.

53 National Conference of Charities and Correction, *Proceedings, 1883* (1884), p. 354.

54 Nicole Rafter, "Chastising the unchaste: social control functions of a women's reformatory, 1894–1931," in *Social Control and the State* eds. S. Cohen and A. Scull (1983), pp. 288–311.

55 As quoted in Rothman, *Conscience and Convenience*, p. 270.

56 William Russell, *The New York Hospital: A History of the Psychiatric Service, 1771–1936* (1945), p. 184.

57 Ibid., p. 244.

58 Ibid., p. 423.

59 Rothman, *The Discovery of the Asylum*, p. 146.

60 Gerald Grob, *Mental Illness and American Society, 1875–1940* (1983), p. 23.
61 Rothman, *Conscience and Convenience*, p. 346.
62 Ibid., p. 349.
63 This predicament was particularly acute in mental hospitals according to Rothman, *Conscience and Convenience*, p. 362.

Chapter 3   Public Welfare in an Age of Social and Economic Crises

1 New York Senate Journal, *Report of the Secretary of the State in 1824 on the Relief and Settlement of the Poor* (1824), p. 950.
2 Massachusetts, *Report of the Commissioners appointed by an order of the house of representatives, Feb. 29, 1832, on the Subject of the Pauper System of the Commonwealth of Massachusetts* (1833), p. 40.
3 Robert Cray contends that, at least in the New York area, some rural villages had also adopted the almshouse, but the policy vacillated. His study seems to verify the idea that, up until the 1820s, most communities dealt with the poor in a variety of ways depending on the circumstances. This including building a poor-house only to abandon its use at a later date. See Robert Cray, *Paupers and Poor Relief in New York City and its Rural Environs, 1700–1830* (1988).
4 Cray, *Paupers and Poor Relief*, pp. 60–5; David Rothman, *The Discovery of the Asylum: Social Order and Disorder in the New Republic* (1971), pp. 32–3.
5 Cray, *Paupers and Poor Relief*, p. 66.
6 Douglass North, *The Economic Growth of the United States, 1790–1860* (1966), p. 51.
7 Cray, *Paupers and Poor Relief*, p. 84. See also Jackson Main, *The Social Structure of Revolutionary America* (1965), pp. 28–30.
8 Even family members in New York had to be forced, by law in 1773, to take responsibility for their relatives. According to Cray, this appears as further evidence of the breakdown in social cohesiveness. See Cray, *Paupers and Poor Relief*, pp. 92–3.
9 Martha Branscombe, *The Courts and the Poor Laws in New York State, 1784–1929* (1943), p. 30.
10 Harold Faulkner asserts that American exports fell from $108,343,150 in 1807 to $22,430,960 in 1808 and imports from

$138,500,000 to $56,990,000. See his *American Economic History* ([1924] 1960), p. 222.

11 Cray, *Paupers and Poor Relief*, pp. 117–24.

12 Massachusetts, *Report of the Committee on the Pauper Laws of this Commonwealth* (1821), p. 9.

13 Clearly the balance between benevolence and punishment was shifting. Those refusing to work were placed in solitary confinement; able-bodied found begging were regarded as disorderly and could be sentenced to the workhouse and hard labor for up to six months. Children under 15 caught begging were also sent to the poorhouse and trained at "useful labor."

14 David Rothman, *The Discovery of the Asylum: Social Order and Disorder in the New Republic* (1971), p. 183 citing New York Senate Document 72 (1853), pp. 52–4.

15 Massachusetts State Board of Charities *First Annual Report* (1865), pp. 326–7.

16 Benjamin Klebaner's work, *Public Poor Relief in America, 1790–1860* ([1951] 1976), pp. 73–99 provides an excellent review of almshouse legislation as it spread throughout the states.

17 Moreover, by providing subsistence independent of participation in private production, particularly during deflationary times, the state would be effectively undermining the position of capital in capital/wage-labor relations. Clearly, the state simply had no business, materially or ideologically, in supporting the poor in such a way at this time.

18 Massachusetts, *Report of the Committee on the Pauper Laws of this Commonwealth* p. 9.

19 New York, *Report on the Select Committee Appointed to Visit Charitable Institutions Supported by the State* (1857), p. 6–7.

20 New York State Governors, *Messages from the Governors* (1909), pp. 760–1.

21 "The causes of pauperism," in New York State Board of Charities, *Annual Report, 1877*, pp. 97–8.

22 Michael Katz, *Poverty and Policy in American History* (1983), pp. 90–133, 259–70.

23 Martha Branscombe, *The Courts and the Poor Laws in New York State*, p. 57. See also Conference of Charities, *Proceedings, 1879* (1879), pp. 202–3.

24 New York City Department of Public Charities and Correction, *Sixteenth Annual Report, 1875* (1876), pp. vii–ix as quoted in David Schneider and Albert Deutsch, *The History of Public Welfare*

in New York State, 1867–1940 (1941), p. 38.

25   Alexander Johnson, *The Almshouse: Construction and Management* (1911), pp. 2–3.

26   US Bureau of the Census, *The Historical Statistics of the United States: Colonial Times to 1970* (1975), p. 135.

27   Schneider and Deutsch, *The History of Public Welfare in New York State*, pp. 54–5.

28   Ibid., pp. 202–4 and New York State Board of Charities, *Forty-sixth Annual Report, 1912*, pp. 138–9; *Forty-seventh Annual Report, 1913*, p. 749.

29   US Census Bureau, *Paupers in Almshouses, 1923* (1925).

30   Branscombe, *The Courts and the Poor Laws in New York State*, p. 176; Schneider and Deutsch, *The History of Public Welfare in New York State*, pp. 240–7.

31   New York State Board of Charities *Annual Report, 1920* (1921), p. 568; *Annual Report, 1921* (1922), p. 397; *Annual Report, 1922* (1923), p. 384.

32   D. K. Bruner, *The Township and Borough System of Relief in Pennsylvania* (unpublished), p. 37 citing state data.

33   Examples of such investigative bodies include The New York City Mayor's Committee on Unemployment formed in 1916 and later, at the national level, The President's Conference on Unemployment in September, 1921.

34   Charles Henderson, *Introduction to the Study of the Dependent, Defective and Delinquent Classes* ([1893] 1901), pp. 74–5.

35   US Bureau of the Census, *Insane and Feeble-Minded in Hospitals and Institutions, 1904* (1906), p. 5.

36   Gerald Grob, *Mental Illness and American Society, 1875–1940* (1983), pp. 109–78; David Rothman, *Conscience and Convenience: The Asylum and its Alternatives in Progressive America* (1980), pp. 324–75.

37   As quoted in Schneider and Deutsch, *The History of Public Welfare in New York State*, p. 61.

38   New York State Board of Charities, *Annual Report, 1874*, pp. 74–8; *Annual Report, 1885*, p. 749 as cited in Schneider and Deutsch, *The History of Public Welfare in New York State*, pp. 64–5.

39   Helen Clarke, *Social Legislation: American Laws Dealing with Family, Child, and Dependent* (1940), p. 275.

40   John Sutton, *Stubborn Children: Controling Delinquency in the United States, 1640–1981* (1988).

41   Schneider and Deutsch, *The History of Public Welfare in New York State*, p. 99.

42   US Bureau of the Census, *Paupers in Almshouses, 1923*, p. 14.

43   Massachusetts State Charities, *Report of the Special Joint Committee Appointed to Investigate the Whole System of the Public Charitable Institutions of the Commonwealth of Massachusetts, 1858* (1859), pp. 4–5.

44   This last codification occurred during unprecedented development in Massachusetts state government and law: an attempt to restore stability to the state following Shay's Rebellion.

45   Robert Kelso, *The History of Public Poor Relief in Massachusetts, 1620–1720* (1922), p. 124.

46   Massachusetts, *Report of the Committee on the Pauper Laws of this Commonwealth*, p. 9.

47   Lawrence Friedman, *A History of American Law* (1973), p. 430.

48   In fact, one way some state governments in the 1870s avoided the legitimation problems of distributing outdoor relief was to have private charities disburse such funds. This way, the state avoided the direct cost of administering disbursements; it reduced the possibility of political corruption; and finally, even if public funds were transferred through such private agencies, symbolically at least, the state was not directly supporting some of its citizens.

49   Gerald Grob, *The State and the Mentally Ill* (1966), p. 240.

Chapter 4   Charting the Advanced-Capitalist State

1   US Bureau of the Census, *The Historical Statistics of the United States: Colonial Times to 1970* (1975), p. 224; US Bureau of Labor Statistics, *Employment and Payrolls, December 1940* Serial No. R1250 (1941), p. 17; Dale Yoder and George Davies, *Depression and Recovery* (1934), p. 36; *Historical Statistics to 1970*, p. 135.

2   See Margaret Weir and Theda Skocpol, "State structures and the possibility for 'Keynesian' responses to the great depression in Sweden, Britain, and the United States," in *Bringing the State Back In*, ed. P. Evans et al. (1985), pp. 107–63.

3   Recent work and debate in the literature suggest that a variety of forces shaped the emergence of state policies following the depression. See Theda Skocpol, "Political response to capitalist crisis: neo-Marxist theories of the state and the case of the New Deal," *Politics and Society*, 10 (1980), pp. 155–201; Weir and

Skocpol, "State Structures;" Jill Quadagno, "Welfare capitalism and the Social Security Act of 1935," *American Sociological Review*, 49 (1984), pp. 632–47; and the exchange of comments between Skocpol and Edward Armenta, "Did capitalists shape social security?" *American Sociological Review*, 50 (1985), pp. 572–5 and Quadagno, "Two models of welfare state development: reply to Skocpol and Armenta," *American Sociological Review*, 50 (1985), pp. 575–8.

4   Stephen Skowronek, *Building a New American State: The Expansion of National Administrative Capacities, 1877–1920* (1982), p. 289.

5   Martin Shefter, "Party, bureaucracy, and political change in the United States," in *Political Parties: Development and Decay*, eds Louis Maisel and Joseph Cooper (1978), pp. 211–66, esp. p. 239.

6   Edward Berkowitz and Kim McQuiad, *Creating the Welfare State* (1980), p. 96.

7   Herbert Stein, *The Fiscal Revolution in America* (1969).

8   This agenda was most clearly stated in the Employment Act of 1946 which committed the federal government to "Promote maximum employment, production and purchasing power."

9   See David Gold, "The rise and fall of the Keynesian coalition," *Kapitaliststate* 6 (1977), pp. 129–61; James O'Connor, *The Fiscal Crisis of the State* (1973); Fred Block, "The ruling class does not rule: notes on the Marxist theory of the state," *Socialist Revolution*, 3 (1977), pp. 6–28 and Sammuel Bowles, David Gordon, and Thomas Weisskopf, *Beyond the Waste Land* (1983).

10 Shefter, "Party, bureaucracy and political change," p. 248.

11 See Mary Ruggie, *The State and Working Women* (1984) for a discussion of a continuum of state intervention from the "liberal welfare model" to the "corporatist welfare model." For a discussion of "American exceptionalism" in welfare state development see Jill Quadagno, *The Transformation of Old Age Security* (1988).

12 Clifford Staples, "The politics of employment-based insurance in the United States," *International Journal of Health Services*, 19 (1989), pp. 415–31.

13 Berkowitz and McQuiad, *Creating the Welfare State*, chapter 7.

14 Ibid., p. 143.

15 US Bureau of the Census, *Statistical Abstract of the United States* (1967), p. 79.

16 J. W. Thompson, R. D. Bass, and M. J. Witkin, "Fifty years of psychiatric services, 1940–1990," *Hospital and Community Psychiatry*, 33 (1982), pp. 711–17.

17 Paul Lerman, *Deinstitutionalization and the Welfare State* (1982), p. 37.

18 Gerald Grob, *Mental Illness and American Society, 1875–1940* (1983), p. 181.

19 Phil Brown, *The Transfer of Care: Psychiatric Deinstitutionalization and its Aftermath* (1985), p. 26.

20 Grob, *Mental Illness and American Society*, pp. 289–90.

21 Thompson et al., "Fifty years of psychiatric services."

22 David Rothman, *Conscience and Convenience: The Asylum and its Alternatives in Progressive America* (1980), pp. 349–60; Grob, *Mental Illness and American Society*, pp. 24–5.

23 Rothman, *Conscience and Convenience*, p. 349.

24 Ibid., pp. 350–1.

25 Grob, *Mental Illness and American Society*, p. 196.

26 American Neurological Association, "Proceedings of 1896," *American Journal of Insanity*, LIII (1896), p. 324.

27 Grob, *Mental Illness and American Society*, p. 325.

28 Rothman, *Conscience and Convenience*, p. 331.

29 Grob, *Mental Illness in American Society*, p. 143.

30 Richard Fox, *So Far Disordered in Mind: Insanity in California, 1870–1930* (1978).

31 Ibid., p. 77.

32 Ibid., p. 81.

33 Carol Warren, *Madwives: Schizophrenic Women in the 1950s* (1987).

34 David Mechanic, *Mental Health and Social Policy* ([1969] 1980); Brown, *The Transfer of Care*.

35 Kenneth Appel, "Presidential address: the present challenge of psychiatry," *American Journal of Psychiatry*, III (1954), pp. 1–7.

36 See American Prison Association, *Proceedings* (1930–1933).

37 US Bureau of the Census, *Historical Statistics to 1970* (1975), p. 420.

38 Blake McKelvey, *American Prisons: A History of Good Intentions* ([1936] 1977), p. 299.

39 Quoted in Frederick Haynes, *The American Prison System* (1939), p. 311, no reference to source.

40 Ibid., p. 318.

41 McKelvey, *American Prisons*, p. 305.

42 Ibid., p. 306.

43 James Bennett, *I Chose Prison* (1970), pp. 89–91.

44 US Bureau of the Census, *Historical Statistics to 1970*, pp. 420, 42.

45 McKelvey, *American Prisons*, pp. 322–35.

46 US Bureau of the Census, *Historical Statistics to 1970*, p. 416.

47 John Sutton, *Stubborn Children: Controlling Delinquency in the United States, 1640–1981* (1988), p. 197.

48 Anthony Platt, *The Child Savers* (1969), p. 50.

49 US Bureau of the Census, *Historical Statistics to 1970*, p. 419.

50 US Bureau of the Census, *Statistical Abstracts* (1930), p. 65, (1940), p. 80; and US Bureau of the Census, *Institutional Popula-tions, 1950* vol. 4, Special Reports, Part 2, chapter C (1953).

51 O. Keller and B. Alper, *Halfway Houses: Community-centered Correction and Treatment* (1970), p. xi.

52 US Bureau of the Census, *Historical Statistics to 1970*, p. 85.

53 US Bureau of the Census, *Institutional Populations, 1950*.

54 Lerman, *Deinstitutionalization*, p. 37.

Chapter 5   Contradictions and Consequences in Post-war Psychiatry

1 Andrew Scull, *Decarceration: Community Treatment and the Deviant – A Radical View* ([1977] 1984), p. 96.

2 Albert Deutsch, *The Shame of the States* (1948), p. 98.

3 Ibid., p. 184.

4 Council of State Governments, *The Mental Health Programs of the Forty-eight States: A Report to the Governors' Conference* (1950), p. 1.

5 Ibid.; and Council of State Governments, *Training and Research in State Mental Health Programs: A Report to the Governors' Conference* (1953).

6 Council of State Governments, *The Mental Health Programs of the Forty-eight States*, p. 30.

7 Council of State Governments, *Training and Research in State Mental Health Programs*, p. 2.

8 Ibid., pp. 4–5.

9 Council of State Governments, *The Mental Health Programs of the Forty-eight States*, p. 43.

10 Ibid., p. 107.

11 Ibid., pp. 109, 117, 118.

12 Ibid., p. 4.

13 Ibid., p. 12.

14 Council of State Governments, Interstate Clearing House on

Mental Health, *State Action in Mental Health, 1956–1957* (1958), p. 1.

15   Ibid., pp. 1–2.

16   See Scull, *Decarceration*; Peter Sedgwick, *Psychopolitics* (1982); Paul Lerman, *Deinstitutionalization and the Welfare State* (1982); and S. P. Segal and U. Aviram, *The Mentally Ill in Community-based Sheltered Care: A Study of Community Care and Social Integration* (1978).

17   See the State of California, *Senate Interim Committee on the Treatment of Mental Illness*, First Partial Report (1956a).

18   It is interesting to note as well how the hospital environment is considered here as potentially curative in light of the emerging critique of the "total institution" during the same time.

19   J. W. Thompson, R. D. Bass, and M. J. Witkin, "Fifty years of psychiatric services, 1940–1990," *Hospital and Community Psychiatry*, 33 (1982), pp. 711–17.

20   Interstate Clearing House on Mental Health, *State Action in Mental Health, 1958–1959* (1960), p. 2.

21   NIMH defines net releases as summing the resident patients at the beginning of the year, plus admissions, and subtracting from this deaths and resident patients at year's end (see M. Kramer, "Psychiatric services and the changing institutional scene, 1950–1985," National Institute of Mental Health Series B, No. 12 (1977), p. 78.

22   J. P. Morrissey and H. H. Goldman, "Care and treatment of the mentally ill in the United States: historical developments and reforms," in *The Law and Mental Health: Research and Policy*, ed. S. A. Shah (1986), pp. 12–27.

23   Reprinted in State of California, *Senate Interim Committee on the Treatment of Mental Illness*, Second Partial Report (1956b), p. 65.

24   Office of Management and Budget, "Historical tables: budget of the United States Government" (1987) and US Bureau of the Census, *Statistical Abstract of the United States* (1960), p. 422.

25   Interstate Clearing House on Mental Health, *State Action in Mental Health, 1958–1959*, p. 2.

26   Morrissey and Goldman, "Care and treatment of the mentally ill in the United States," p. 21.

27   Joint Commission on Mental Illness and Health, *Action for Mental Health: Final Report of Joint Commission on Mental Illness and Health* (1961).

28   Ibid., pp. xv, xvii.

29 R. H. Connery, C. H. Blackstrom, D. R. Deewer, J. R. Friedman et al., *The Politics of Mental Health* (1968); D. A. Felicetti, *Mental Health and Retardation Politics: The Mind Lobbies in Congress* (1975); and Henry Foley, *Community Mental Health Legislation: The Formative Process* (1975).

30 David Mechanic, *Mental Health and Social Policy* ([1969] 1980), p. 82.

31 The only significant objection to the original legislation came from the American Medical Association which felt that provisions for staffing grants constituted a movement toward "socialized" medicine. The provision was subsequently dropped from the final version (see Foley, *Community Mental Health Legislation*).

32 Ibid., p. 83.

33 See Kramer, "Psychiatric services and the changing institutional scene;" and Laura Milazzo-Sayre, "Changes in the age, sex, and diagnostic composition of the resident population of state and county mental hospitals, United States 1965–1975," National Institute of Mental Health Statistical Note No. 146. (1978).

34 Milazzo-Sayre, "Changes in the age, sex, and diagnostic composition;" and R. W. Redick and M. J. Witkin, "State and county mental hospitals, United States, 1979–80 and 1980–81," National Institute of Mental Health Statistical Note No. 165 (1983a).

35 Michael Witkin, "Trends in patient care episodes in mental health facilities, 1955–1977," National Institute of Mental Health Statistical Note No. 107. (1980).

36 U. Aviram, L. S. Syme, and J. B. Cohen, "The effects of policies and programs on the reduction of mental hospitalization," *Social Science and Medicine*, 10 (1976), pp. 571–7; Joseph Morrissey, "Deinstitutionalizing the mentally ill: process, outcomes, and new directions," in *Deviance and Mental Illness*, ed. W. Gove (1982), pp. 147–76; and C. J. Smith and R. Q. Hanham, "Deinstitutionalization of the mentally ill: a time path analysis of American states, 1955–1975," *Social Science and Medicine*, 15 (1981), pp. 361–81.

37 J. P. Morrissey, M. J. Witkin, R. W. Manderscheid, and H. E. Bethel, "Trends by state in the capacity and volume of inpatient services, state and county mental hospitals, United States, 1976–1980," Series CN, No. 10 (1986).

Chapter 6   Public Policy under the Liberal Welfare State

1   Andrew Scull, *Decarceration: Community Treatment and the Deviant – A Radical View* ([1977] 1984).
2   See James O'Connor, *The Fiscal Crisis of the State* (1973).
3   Harold Vatter, *The US Economy in the 1950s; An Economic History* (1963).
4   See Herbert Stein, *The Fiscal Revolution in America* (1969). While Kennedy had campaigned and took office holding to a policy of "fiscal responsibility," not long after he was espousing the virtues of Keynesian macroeconomic policies as in his 1962 Yale Commencement Address.
5   Robert Gordon, *Economic Instability and Growth: The American Record* (1974), p. 147.
6   Walter Heller, *New Dimensions of Political Economy* (1966); R. B. DuBoff and E. S. Herman, "The new economics: handmaiden of inspired truth," *The Review of Radical Political Economics*, IV (1972), pp. 54–84.
7   Gordon, *Economic Instability*, p. 140.
8   Arthur Okun, "Measuring the impact of the 1964 tax reduction," in *Perspectives on Economic Growth*, ed. W. Heller (1968), pp. 25–49.
9   Gordon, *Economic Instability*, p. 146.
10 Martin Shefter "Party, bureaucracy, and political change in the United States," in *Political Parties: Development and Decay*, eds Louis Maisel and Joseph Cooper (1978), p. 245; see also Frances Piven and Richard Cloward, *Regulating the Poor: the Functions of Public Welfare* (1974).
11 Gordon, *Economic Instability*, p. 168.
12 David Mechanic, *Mental Health and Social Policy* ([1969] 1980), p. 83.
13 F. D. Chu and S. Trotter, *The Madness Establishment* (1974).
14 Michael Dear and Jennifer Wolch, *Landscapes of Despair: From Deinstitutionalization to Homelessness* (1987).
15 Bruce Vladeck, *Unloving Care: The Nursing Home Tragedy* (1980).
16 Burton Dunlop, *The Growth of Nursing Home Care* (1979), pp. 60, 106.
17 Paul Lerman, *Deinstitutionalization and the Welfare State* (1982), p. 215.

18 As reported by Dunlop, *The Growth of Nursing Home Care*, pp. 8–9; D. R. Waldo and H. C. Lazenby, "Demographic characteristics and health care use and expenditures by the aged in the United States, 1977–1984," *Health Care Financing Review*, 6 (1984), pp. 1–22.

19 Richard Redick, "Patterns in the use of nursing homes by the aged mentally ill," National Institute of Mental Health Statistical Note No. 107 (1974).

20 US General Accounting Office, *Returning the Mentally Disabled to the Community: Government Needs to Do More* (1977), p. 11.

21 Ibid., p. 11.

22 Waldo and Lazenby, "Demographic characteristics."

23 Redick, "Patterns in the use of nursing homes."

24 Jeff Blyskal, "Grey gold," *Forbes* (1981).

25 For a particularly moving account of this trend see Timothy Diamond, *The Making of Gray Gold: The Industrialization of Nursing Home Care* (draft manuscript).

26 Martin Cosgrove, "The hospital management industry: update on the legislative front," (unpublished research report, 1981), p. 5.

27 See R. M. Emerson, E. B. Rochford, and L. L. Shaw, "Economics and enterprise in board and care homes for the mentally ill," *American Behavioral Scientist*, 24 (1981), pp. 771–85 and "The micropolitics of trouble in a psychiatric board and care facility," *Urban Life*, 12 (1983), pp. 349–67; Lerman, *Deinstitutionalization*, pp. 46–7; Phil Brown, *The Transfer of Care: Psychiatric Deinstitutionalization and its Aftermath* (1985), pp. 99–101.

28 S. P. Segal and U. Aviram, *The Mentally Ill in Community-based Sheltered Care: A Study of Community Care and Social Integration* (1978), p. 137.

29 Lerman, *Deinstitutionalization*, pp. 47–8.

30 Brown, *The Transfer of Care*, p. 100.

31 Ibid., p. 101.

32 US Department of Justice, *Sourcebook of Criminal Justice Statistics* (1985), p. 531.

33 Federal Bureau of Investigation, *Crime in the United States: Uniform Crime Reports* (1957–1967).

34 US Bureau of the Census, *The Historical Statistics of the United States: Colonial Times to 1970* (1975), pp. 413, 415.

35 US Bureau of the Census, *Social Indicators, 1976* (1977), p. 24. One colleague suggested the reduction might have been a function of the Vietnam War. However, the US had limited troop

involvement in the early 1960s. While data on military personnel for the period indicates that the rate per 1,000 in the population serving did rise from 13.5 to 15.0 that year, it accelerated later in the decade, peaking in 1968 at 17.7 according to US Bureau of the Census, *Statistical Abstract of the United States* (1985), p. 340. Given the dramatic fall in incarceration rates in 1962, it would appear that the affect of military service would be minor.

36 Ronald Berkman, *Opening the Gates: The Rise of the Prisoners' Movement* (1979).

37 Quoted in American Correctional Association, *Proceedings of the Eighty-ninth Annual Congress of Correction* (1958), p. 9.

38 US Bureau of the Census, *Historical Statistics to 1970* (1975), pp. 420–1.

39 President's Commission on Law Enforcement and the Administration of Justice, *The Challenge of Crime in a Free Society* (1967).

40 Ibid., pp. 7, 165.

41 Ibid., p. 165.

42 H. G. Moeller, "Community-based correctional services," in *Handbook of Criminology*, ed. D. Glaser (1974), pp. 895–907.

43 Edward Lemert and Forrest Dill, *Offenders in the Community* (1978); R. Smith, *A Quiet Revolution – Probation Subsidy* (1972), p. 48.

44 US Bureau of the Census, *Historical Statistics to 1970* (1975), p. 419; US Social Security Administration, *Social Security Bulletin* (1980), p. 65. The *Historical Statistics* text cautions the reader concerning the comparability of these numbers given that the 1960 and 1970 figures represent 25 percent and 20 percent respectively and that changes in classifications have also occurred. Since no other source of national data exist on such facilities, these estimates must remain as baselines for this period. Data on juvenile facilities were more systematically collected after 1970.

45 President's Commission, *The Challenge of Crime in a Free Society*, p. 45.

46 US Senate Committee on the Judiciary, *Ford Administration Stifles Juvenile Justice Policy* (1975), p. 2.

47 See Meda Chesney-Lind, "Judicial paternalism and the female status offender: training women to know their place," *Crime and Delinquency*, 23 (1977), pp. 121–30 and my own "Toward a structural perspective on gender bias in the juvenile court," *Sociological Perspectives*, 27 (1984), pp. 349–67 and "Law and social control in juvenile justice dispositions," *Journal of Research in*

Crime and Delinquency, 24 (1987b), pp. 7–22.

48 US Bureau of the Census, *Children in Custody* (1974, 1979); and Barry Krisberg and Ira Schwartz, "Rethinking juvenile justice," *Crime and Delinquency*, 29 (1983), pp. 333–64.

49 Francis Cullen and Karen Gilbert, *Reaffirming Rehabilitation* (1982), p. 93.

50 Robert Martinson, "What works? Questions and answers about prison reform," *The Public Interest*, 35 (1974), pp. 22–54.

51 Francis Allen, *The Decline of the Rehabilitative Ideal: Penal Policy and Social Purpose* (1981).

52 US Department of Justice, *Sourcebook of Criminal Justice Statistics* (1985), p. 531.

53 J. Mullen, K. J. Chabotar, and D. M. Carrow, *The Privatization of Corrections* (1985).

54 Joan Mullen, "Corrections and the private sector," in *National Institute of Justice Reports* (1985), pp. 2–7.

55 G. M. Henry, "Inside job: cheery voices from behind bars," *Time* (1986).

56 Mullen, "Corrections and the private sector," p. 3.

57 E. F. Hutton, *Innovative Alternatives to Traditional Jail Financing* (1984).

58 US Congress Joint Economic Committee, "Privatization of prison construction in New York." Hearing of December 5, 1984 (1985), p. 2.

59 Mullen, "Corrections in the private sector," p. 4.

60 The surveys define correctional facility as (a) detention centers; (b) shelters; (c) reception or diagnostic centers; (d) training schools; (e) ranches, forestry camps and farms; (f) halfway houses and group homes, US Bureau of the Census, *Children in Custody* (1974), p. 26.

61 Krisberg and Schwartz, "Rethinking juvenile justice."

62 J. A. Arnaud and T. C. Mack, "The deinstitutionalization of status offenders in Massachusetts: the role of the private sector," in *Neither Angels Nor Thieves: Studies in the Deinstitutionalization of Status Offenders*, eds J. F. Handler and J. Zatz (1982), pp. 372–419.

63 Ibid., p. 353.

64 Peter Conrad and Joseph Schneider, *Deviance and Medicalization: From Badness to Sickness* (1980); and Malcolm Spector, "Beyond crime: seven methods to control troublesome rascals," in *Law and Deviance*, ed. H. L. Ross (1981), pp. 127–58.

65 Carol Warren, "New forms of social control: the myth of

deinstitutionalization," *American Behavioral Scientist*, 25 (1981), pp. 724–40; Patricia Guttridge and Carol Warren, "Adolescent psychiatric hospitalization and social control," in *Mental Health and Criminal Justice* ed. L. Teplin (1984), pp. 119–37.

66   See I. Schwartz, M. Jackson-Beeck, and R. Anderson, "The 'hidden' system of juvenile control," *Crime and Delinquency*, 30 (1984), pp. 371–85; William Staples and Carol Warren, "Mental health and adolescent social control," in *Research in Law, Deviance and Social Control: A Research Annual*, eds S. Spitzer and A. Scull (1988), pp. 113–26; Carol Warren and William Staples, "Fieldwork in forbidden terrain: the state, privatization and human subjects regulations," *The American Sociologist* vol. 20 3 Fall (1989), pp. 263–77.

67   American Psychiatric Association, *Diagnostic and Statistical Manual of Mental Disorders*, third edition (1980).

68   Ibid., pp. 45–6.

69   National Institute of Mental Health, "Trends in age specific admissions rates to public and private psychiatric hospitals," unpublished raw data (1985).

70   National Association of Private Psychiatric Hospitals, *Membership Survey*, unpublished (1983).

71   Patricia Guttridge, *Psychiatric and Non-psychiatric Factors Affecting Mental Hospitalization of Juveniles*, unpublished doctoral dissertation (1981); Guttridge and Warren, "Adolescent psychiatric hospitalization and social control."

72   The private hospitals were also more likely to have voluntary juvenile inpatients and the public hospital to have involuntary commitments. In California, as in most other states, incarceration in a psychiatric hospital may occur, for adults, on a voluntary or involuntary basis. While juveniles may be involuntarily committed to psychiatric institutions under the same legislation as for adults, for juveniles, the term "voluntary" refers to being volunteered by parents or guardian; it is only very rarely that juveniles either do, or are permitted by law to, sign themselves into a psychiatric institution. As with the private juvenile correctional facilities covered above, private psychiatric hospitals have higher rates of voluntary placement than their public sector counterparts.

73   Schwartz, et al., "The 'hidden' system of juvenile control."

74   Richard Redick and Michael Witkin, "State and county mental hospitals, United States, 1979–80 and 1980–81," National Insti-

tute of Mental Health Statistical Note No. 165 (1983a).

75   J. W. Thompson, R. D. Bass, and M. J. Witkin, "Fifty years of psychiatric services, 1940–1990," *Hospital and Community Psychiatry*, 33 (1982), p. 712.

76   Modern Health Care, "1984 multi-unit providers," *Modern Health Care* 14 (1984), pp. 65–178.

77   A. Levenson, "The for-profit system," in *The New Economics and Psychiatric Care* ed. S. Sharfstein and A. Beigel (1985), pp. 151–63.

78   Thompson, Bass, and Witkin, "Fifty Years of Psychiatric Services."

79   Richard Redick and Michael Witkin, "Residential treatment centers for emotionally disturbed children in the United States, 1977–1980," National Institute of Mental Health Statistical Note No. 162 (1983b).

80   Elyce Zenoff and Allan Zients, "If civil commitment is the answer for children, what are the questions?," *The George Washington Late Review*, 51 (1983), pp. 171–214.

81   Redick and Witkin, "Residential treatment centers for emotionally disturbed children."

82   D. R. Buckholt and J. W. Gubrium, *Caretakers: Treating Emotionally Disturbed Children* (1979).

83   Krisberg and Schwartz, "Rethinking juvenile justice," p. 361.

84   National Association of Private Psychiatric Hospitals, *Membership Survey*, unpublished (1983).

Chapter 7   The Evolution of the State Apparatus

1   Alexis de Tocqueville, *On Democracy, Revolution, and Society*, eds J. Stone and S. Mennell (1980), pp. 362–3.

2   See my "Restitution as a sanction in juvenile court," *Crime and Delinquency*, 32 (1986) pp. 177–85, as an example of another social control policy with seemingly universal policy appeal.

3   See Mary Ruggie, *The State and Working Women* (1984), pp. 14–15.

4   John Keane, Introduction to *Contradictions of the Welfare State* by C. Offe, ed. J. Keane (1984), pp. 11–34.

5   This, of course, was part of Scull's *Decarceration* thesis. My own analysis suggests however that the convoluted path of history between the mid-1950s and the 1980s defies any "reading off" of

a "fiscal crisis" thesis. The strategies and policies of the Kennedy administration and the abrupt reversal in adult prison rates in the early 1970s are just two instances that demand a more flexible analysis – one I believe I have offered.

6 John Lowman, Robert Menzies, and T. S. Palys, "Introduction: transcarceration and the modern state of penality," in *Transcarceration: Essays in the Sociology of Social Control*, ed J. Lowman, R. Menzies, and T. Palys (1987), pp. 1–26, esp. p. 6.

7 For example, production techniques originating in the factory were imported into the prison in the nineteenth century, while the use of electroconvulsive therapy, the trademark of the public insane asylum, is now favored by private psychiatric hospitals.

8 That is, by pursuing a policy of public institutionalization, the state engages in the systematic removal of individuals from any possibility of participating in the nexus of commodity exchange relations. In Claus Offe's words, these individuals have been "decommodified," thus the state must subsidize their daily existence. This fact accounts, in part, for the extensive use of labor in institutions. According to Offe, welfare state policies reflect a constant tension between "commodification," "decommodification," and "recommodification." See Claus Offe, *Contradictions of the Welfare State*, ed. J. Keane (1984).

9 Moreover, the privatization of once-public care and control institutions has a number of important social consequences, both for social order and for social research. These consequences might be summarized as the social invisibility of clientele which takes two forms: one is the invisibility of the everyday lives of clientele, while the other is the invisibility of entire sectors of the system, excluding them from public accountability and policy debate. See Carol Warren and William Staples, "Fieldwork in forbidden terrain: the state, privatization and human subjects regulations," *The American Sociologist* vol. 20 3 Fall (1989), pp. 263–77.

Appendix: Concepts, Data, and Sources

1 Stanley Cohen, *Visions of Social Control* (1985), p. 2.
2 Nanette Davis and Bo Anderson, *Social Control: The Production of Deviance in the Modern State* (1983), pp. 35–6.
3 Erving Goffman, *Asylums* (1961).

References

Allen, Francis, *The Decline of the Rehabilitative Ideal: Penal Policy and Social Purpose* (New Haven: Yale University Press, 1981).

American Correctional Association, *Proceedings of the Eighty-ninth Annual Congress of Correction* (1958).

American Neurological Association, "Proceedings of 1896," *American Journal of Insanity*, LIII (1896).

American Prison Association, *Proceedings* (1930–1933).

American Psychiatric Association, *Diagnostic and Statistical Manual of Mental Disorders*, third edition (Washington DC: American Psychiatric Association, 1980).

Appel, Kenneth, "Presidential address: the present challenge of psychiatry," *American Journal of Psychiatry*, III (1954), pp. 1–7.

Arnaud, J. A., and Mack, T. C. "The deinstitutionalization of status offenders in Massachusetts: the role of the private sector," in *Neither Angels Nor Thieves: Studies in the Deinstitutionalization of Status Offenders*, eds J. F. Handler and J. Zatz (Washington DC: National Academy, 1982), pp. 372–419.

Aviram, U., Syme, L. S., and Cohen, J. B., "The effects of policies and programs on the reduction of mental hospitalization," *Social Science and Medicine*, 10 (1976), pp. 571–7.

Barnes, Harry, *A History of the Penal, Reformatory, and Correctional Institutions of the State of New Jersey* (Trenton, NJ: MacCrellish and Quigley, 1918).

——*The Evolution of Penology in Pennsylvania: A Study in American Social History* (Indianapolis: Bobbs-Merrill, 1927).

Beaumont, Gustave de, and Tocqueville, Alexis de, *On the Penitentiary System of the United States and its Application in France*, tr. Francis Lieber (Philadelphia: Carey Lea and Blanchard, 1833).

Bennett, James, *I Chose Prison* (New York: Knopf, 1970).

Berkman, Ronald, *Opening the Gates: The Rise of the Prisoners'*

Movement (Lexington, MA: Heath, 1979).

Berkowitz, Edward and McQuiad, Kim, *Creating the Welfare State* (New York: Praeger, 1980).

Block, Fred, "The ruling class does not rule: notes on the Marxist theory of the state," *Socialist Revolution*, 3 (1977) pp. 6–28.

Blyskal, Jeff, "Grey gold," *Forbes*, November 23, 1981.

Bowles, Sammuel, Gordon, David, and Weisskopf, Thomas, *Beyond the Waste Land* (New York: Doubleday, 1983).

Branscombe, Martha, *The Courts and the Poor Laws in New York State, 1784–1929* (Chicago: University of Chicago Press, 1943).

Breckinridge, Sophonisba, *Public Welfare Administration in the United States* (Chicago: University of Chicago Press, 1927).

Brown, Phil, *The Transfer of Care: Psychiatric Deinstitutionalization and its Aftermath* (London: Routledge and Kegan Paul, 1985).

Bruner, D. K., *The Township and Borough System of Relief in Pennsylvania*, (unpublished doctoral dissertation, University of Pennsylvania, 1937).

Buckholt, D. R., and Gubrium, J. W., *Caretakers: Treating Emotionally Disturbed Children* (Beverly Hills, CA: Sage, 1979).

Burawoy, Michael, "Karl Marx and the satanic mills: factory politics under early capitalism in England, the United States, and Russia," *American Journal of Sociology* 90 (1984), pp. 247–82.

Chesney-Lind, Meda, "Judicial paternalism and the female status offender: training women to know their place," *Crime and Delinquency*, 23 (1977), pp. 121–30.

Chu, F. D., and Trotter, S., *The Madness Establishment* (New York: Grossman, 1974).

Clark, Gordon, and Dear, Michael, *State Apparatus: Structures and Language of Legitimacy* (Boston: Allen and Unwin, 1984).

Clarke, Helen, *Social Legislation: American Laws Dealing with Family, Child and Dependent* (New York: Appleton-Century, 1940).

Cohen, Stanley, *Visions of Social Control* (Cambridge, UK: Polity, 1985).

Cohen, Stanley, and Scull, Andrew, *Social Control and the State* (New York: St Martin's, 1983).

Commissioner of Labor, *Convict Labor, 1886*. Second Annual Report of the Commissioner of Labor (Washington DC: US Government Printing Office, 1887).

Commons, John, *History of Labor in the United States, 1895–1932* (New York: Kelley [1921] 1966).

Conference of Charities, *Proceedings, 1879* (Boston, 1879).

Connery, R. H., Blackstrom, C. H., Deewer, D. R., Friedman, J. R., Krull, M., Marden, R. H., McCleskey, C., Meekison, P., and Morgan, J. A., *The Politics of Mental Health* (New York: Columbia University Press, 1968).

Conrad, Peter, and Schneider, Joseph, *Deviance and Medicalization: From Badness to Sickness* (St Louis, MO: C. V. Mosby, 1980).

Cosgrove, Martin, "The hospital management industry: update on the legislative front," (unpublished research report, Los Angeles: Bateman, Eichler, Hill Richards, 1981).

Council of State Governments, *The Mental Health Programs of the Forty-eight States: A Report to the Governors' Conference* (Chicago: Council of State Governments, 1950).

——*Training and Research in State Mental Health Programs: A Report to the Governors' Conference* (Chicago: Council of State Governments, 1953).

——Interstate Clearing House on Mental Health, *State Action in Mental Health, 1956–1957* (Chicago: Council of State Governments, 1958).

——Interstate Clearing House on Mental Health, *State Action in Mental Health, 1958–1959* (Chicago: Council of State Governments, 1960).

Cray, Robert, *Paupers and Poor Relief in New York City and its Rural Environs, 1700–1830* (Philadelphia: Temple University Press), 1988.

Cullen, Francis, and Gilbert, Karen, *Reaffirming Rehabilitation* (Cincinnati, OH: Anderson, 1982).

Davis, Nanette, and Anderson, Bo, *Social Control: The Production of Deviance in the Modern State* (New York: Irvington, 1983).

Dear, Michael, and Wolch, Jennifer, *Landscapes of Despair: From Deinstitutionalization to Homelessness* (Princeton: Princeton University Press, 1987).

Deutsch, Albert, *The Shame of the States* (New York: Harcourt, Brace, 1948).

Diamond, Timothy, *The Making of Gray Gold: The Industrialization of Nursing Home Care*, draft manuscript (Department of Sociology, California State University, Los Angeles, 1988).

DuBoff, R. B., and Herman, E. S., "The new economics: handmaiden of inspired truth," *The Review of Radical Political Economics*, IV (1972), pp. 54–84.

Dumm, Thomas, *Democracy and Punishment: Disciplinary Origins of the*

United States (Madison: University of Wisconsin Press, 1987).

Dunlop, Burton, *The Growth of Nursing Home Care* (Lexington, MA: Heath, 1979).

Hutton, E. F., *Innovative Alternatives to Traditional Jail Financing* (New York: E. F. Hutton and Co., 1984).

Emerson, R. M., Rochford, E. B., and Shaw, L. L., "Economics and enterprise in board and care homes for the mentally ill," *American Behavioral Scientist*, 24 (1981), pp. 771–85.

——"The micropolitics of trouble in a psychiatric board and care facility," *Urban Life*, 12 (1983), pp. 349–67.

Faulkner, Harold, *American Economic History* (New York: Harpers, [1924] 1960).

Federal Bureau of Investigation, *Crime in the United States: Uniform Crime Reports* (Washington DC: US Government Printing Office, 1957–1967).

Felicetti, D. A., *Mental Health and Retardation Politics: The Mind Lobbies in Congress* (New York: Praeger, 1975).

Foley, Henry, *Community Mental Health Legislation: The Formative Process* (Lexington, MA: Heath, 1975).

Foucault, Michel, *Discipline and Punish*, tr. A. M. Sheridan (New York: Patheon, 1977).

——*Madness and Civilization: A History of Insanity in the Age of Reason*, tr. R. Howard (New York: Vintage, [1965] 1973).

Fox, Richard, *So Far Disordered in Mind: Insanity in California, 1870–1930* (Berkeley: University of California Press, 1978).

Friedman, Lawrence, *A History of American Law* (New York: Simon and Schuster, 1973).

Giddens, Anthony, *The Constitution of Society* (Berkeley and Los Angeles: University of California Press, 1984).

Gill, H. B., "The prison labor problem," in *Prisons of Tomorrow* eds E. H. Sutherland and T. Sellin (Philadelphia: The Annals of the American Academy of Political and Social Science, 1931), pp. 83–101.

Goffman, Erving, *Asylums* (Garden City, NJ: Doubleday Anchor, 1961).

Gold, David, "The rise and fall of the Keynesian coalition," *Kapitalistate* 6 (1977), pp. 129–61.

Gordon, Robert, *Economic Instability and Growth: The American Record* (New York: Harper and Row, 1974).

Grob, Gerald, *Mental Illness and American Society, 1875–1940* (Princeton, NJ: Princeton University Press, 1983).

——*The State and the Mentally Ill* (Chapel Hill: University of North Carolina Press, 1966).

Guttridge, Patricia, *Psychiatric and Non-psychiatric Factors Affecting Mental Hospitalization of Juveniles* (unpublished doctoral dissertation, (Department of Sociology, University of Southern California, 1981).

Guttridge, P., and Warren, C., "Adolescent psychiatric hospitalization and social control," in *Mental Health and Criminal Justice* ed. L. Teplin (Beverly Hills, CA: Sage, 1984), pp. 119–37.

Habermas, Jurgen, *Legitimation Crisis*, tr. T. McCarthy (Boston: Beacon Press, 1973).

Handlin, Oscar and Mary Flug *Commonwealth – A Study of the Role of Government in the American Economy: Massachusetts, 1774–1861* (Cambridge, MA: Harvard University Press, [1947] 1969).

Hartz, Louis, *Economic Policy and Democratic Thought: Pennsylvania, 1776–1860* (Cambridge, MA: Harvard University Press, 1948).

Haynes, Frederick, *The American Prison System* (New York: McGraw-Hill, 1939).

Heller, Walter, *New Dimensions of Political Economy* (Cambridge, MA: Harvard University Press, 1966).

Henderson, Charles, *Introduction to the Study of the Dependent, Defective and Delinquent Classes* (Boston: Heath, [1893] 1901).

Henry, G. M., "Inside job: cheery voices from behind bars," *Time*, May 12, 1986.

Hindus, Michael, *Prison and Plantation: Crime, Justice, and Authority in Massachusetts and South Carolina, 1767–1878* (Chapel Hill: University of North Carolina Press, 1980).

Ignatieff, Michael, *A Just Measure of Pain: The Penitentiary in the Industrial Revolution, 1750–1850* (New York: Patheon, 1978).

Inspectors of the Eastern Penitentiary (Pennsylvania), *Annual Reports* (Philadelphia, 1837–1880).

Inspectors of the Western Penitentiary (Pennsylvania), *Annual Report* (Philadelphia, 1867).

Ives, George, *A History of Penal Methods* (New York: Stokes, 1914).

Johnson, Alexander, *The Almshouse: Construction and Management* (New York: Russell Sage Foundation, 1911).

Joint Commission on Mental Illness and Health, *Action for Mental Health: Final Report of Joint Commission on Mental Illness and Health* (New York: Basic, 1961).

Katz, Michael, *Poverty and Policy in American History* (New York: Academic Press, 1983).

186   *References*

Keane, John, Introduction to *Contradictions of the Welfare State* by C. Offe ed. J. Keane (Cambridge, MA: MIT Press, 1984), pp. 11–34.

Keller, O., and Alper, B., *Halfway Houses: Community-centered Correction and Treatment* (Lexington, MA: Heath, 1970).

Kelso, Robert, *The History of Public Poor Relief in Massachusetts, 1620–1720* (Boston: Houghton Mifflin, 1922).

Klebaner, Benjamin, *Public Poor Relief in America, 1790–1860* (New York: Arne, [1951] 1976).

Kramer, M., "Psychiatric services and the changing institutional scene, 1950–1985," National Institute of Mental Health Series B, No. 12 (Washington DC: US Government Printing Office, 1977).

Krisberg, Barry, and Schwartz, Ira, "Rethinking juvenile justice," *Crime and Delinquency*, 29 (1983), pp. 333–64.

Lasch, Christopher, *The World of Nations* (New York: Vintage, 1974).

Leiby, James, *Charity and Correction in New Jersey* (New Brunswick, NJ: Rutgers University Press, 1967).

Lemert, Edward, and Dill, Forrest, *Offenders in the Community* (Lexington, MA: Heath, 1978).

Lerman, Paul, *Deinstitutionalization and the Welfare State* (New Brunswick, NJ: Rutgers University Press, 1982).

Levenson, A., "The for-profit system," in *The New Economics and Psychiatric Care* ed. S. Sharfstein and A. Beigel (Washington, DC: American Psychiatric Press, 1985), pp. 151–63.

Lewis, Orlando, *The Development of American Prisons and Prison Customs, 1776–1845* (Albany: Prison Association of New York (1922) 1967).

Lodge, Henry Cabot, *The Federalist: A Commentary on the Constitution of the United States* (New York: G. P. Putnam's Sons, 1883).

Lowman, John, Menzies, Robert, and Palys, T. S., "Introduction: transcarceration and the modern state of penality," in *Transcarceration: Essays in the Sociology of Social Control* eds J. Lowman, R. Menzies, and T. Palys (Aldershot, UK: Grower, 1987), pp. 1–26.

McKelvey, Blake, *American Prisons: A History of Good Intentions* (Montclair, NJ: Patterson Smith, [1936] 1977).

Main, Jackson, *The Social Structure of Revolutionary America* (Princeton: Princeton University Press, 1965).

Mann, Michael, "The autonomous power of the state: its origins, mechanisms and results," *Archives européennes de sociologie* (1984), pp. 185–213.

Martinson, Robert, "What works? Questions and answers about

prison reform," *The Public Interest*, 35 (1974), pp. 22–54.

Massachusetts, *Report of the Committee on the Pauper Laws of this Commonwealth* (Boston, 1821).

——*Report of the Commissioners appointed by an order of the house of representatives, Feb. 29, 1832, on the Subject of the Pauper System of the Commonwealth of Massachusetts* (Boston, 1833).

Massachusetts State Charities, *Report of the Special Joint Committee Appointed to Investigate the Whole System of the Public Charitable Institutions of the Commonwealth of Massachussets, 1858* (Boston, 1859).

Massachusetts State Board of Charities, *First Annual Report* (Boston, 1865).

Mechanic, David, *Mental Health and Social Policy* (Englewood Cliffs, NJ: Prentice-Hall, [1969] 1980).

Melossi, Dario, and Parvarini, Massimo, *The Prison and the Factory: Origins of the Penitentiary System*, tr. G. Cousin (Totowa, NJ: Barnes and Noble, 1978).

Messinger, S., Berecochea, J. E., Rauma, D., and Berk, R. A., "The foundations of parole in California," *Law and Society Review* 19 (1985), pp. 69–106.

Milazzo-Sayre, Laura, "Changes in the age, sex, and diagnostic composition of the resident population of state and county mental hospitals, United States 1965–1975," National Institute of Mental Health Statistical Note No. 146. (Rockville, MD: NIMH, 1978).

Mittleman, E. B., "Prison labor in the United States," in *A History of Labor in the United States, 1895–1932*, ed. J. R. Common (New York: Kelley, [1921] 1966), pp. 327–54.

Modern Health Care, "1984 Multi-unit providers," *Modern Health Care* 14 (1984), pp. 65–178.

Moeller, H. G., "Community-based correctional services," in *Handbook of Criminology*, ed. D. Glaser (Chicago: Rand McNally, 1974), pp. 895–907.

Mohler, H. C., "Convict labor policies," *Journal of Criminal Law and Criminology* 4 (1925), pp. 557–73.

Morrissey, Joseph, "Deinstitutionalizing the mentally ill: process, outcomes, and new directions," in *Deviance and Mental Illness* ed. W. Gove (Beverly Hills, CA: Sage, 1982), pp. 147–76.

Morrissey, J. P., and Goldman, H. H., "Care and treatment of the mentally ill in the United States: historical developments and reforms," in *The Law and Mental Health: Research and Policy* ed. S. A. Shah (Beverly Hills, CA: Sage, 1986), pp. 12–27.

Morrissey, J. P., Witkin, M. J., Manderscheid, R. W., and Bethel, H. E., "Trends by state in the capacity and volume of inpatient services, state and county mental hospitals, United States, 1976–1980," Series CN, No. 10 (Washington DC: US Government Printing Office, 1986).

Mullen, Joan, "Corrections and the private sector," in *National Institute of Justice Reports*, US Department of Justice, National Institute of Justice (Washington DC: Government Printing Office, 1985), pp. 2–7.

Mullen, J., Chabotar, K. J., and Carrow, D. M., *The Privatization of Corrections*, US Department of Justice, National Institute of Justice (Washington: US Government Printing Office, 1985).

National Association of Private Psychiatric Hospitals, *Membership Survey*, unpublished (Washington DC, 1983).

National Conference of Charities and Correction, *Proceedings, 1883* (Madison WI, 1884).

National Institute of Mental Health, "Trends in age specific admissions rates to public and private psychiatric hospitals," unpublished raw data (Rockville, MD: NIMH, 1985).

National Prison Association, *First Annual Report* (New York: National Prison Association, 1884).

National Prison Association, *Proceedings of the National Prison Congress* (Chicago: Donnelley, 1887).

Nettles, C. P., *The Emergence of a National Economy, 1775–1815* (New York: Holt, Rinehart and Winston, 1964).

New York, *Report on the Select Committee Appointed to Visit Charitable Institutions Supported by the State* (Albany, 1857).

New York City Department of Public Charities and Correction, *Sixteenth Annual Report, 1875* (New York, 1876).

New York Senate Journal, *Report of the Secretary of the State in 1824 on the Relief and Settlement of the Poor* (Albany, 1824).

New York State Board of Charities, *Annual Reports* (Albany, 1874–1923).

New York State Governors, *Messages from the Governors* (Albany, 1909).

North, Douglass, *The Economic Growth of the United States, 1790–1860* (New York: Norton, 1966).

O'Connor, James, *The Fiscal Crisis of the State* (New York: St Martin's, 1973).

Offe, Claus, *Contradictions of the Welfare State*, ed. J. Keane (Cambridge, MA: MIT Press, 1984).

Office of Management and Budget, Historical Tables: Budget of the United States Government (Washington: US Government Printing Office, 1987).

Okun, Arthur, "Measuring the impact of the 1964 tax reduction," in *Perspectives on Economic Growth*, ed. W. Heller (New York: Vintage, 1968), pp. 25–49.

Piven, Frances, and Cloward, Richard, *Regulating the Poor: the Functions of Public Welfare* (New York: Pantheon, 1974).

Platt, Anthony, *The Child Savers* (Chicago: University of Chicago Press, 1969).

President's Commission on Law Enforcement and the Administration of Justice, *The Challenge of Crime in a Free Society* (Washington DC: US Government Printing Office, 1967).

Quadagno, Jill, *The Transformation of Old Age Security* (Chicago: University of Chicago Press, 1988).

——"Welfare capitalism and the Social Security Act of 1935," *American Sociological Review*, 49 (1984), pp. 632–47.

——"Two models of welfare state development: reply to Skocpol and Armenta," *American Sociological Review*, 50 (1985), pp. 575–78.

Rafter, Nicole, "Chastising the unchaste: social control functions of a women's reformatory, 1894–1931," in *Social Control and the State* eds S. Cohen and A. Scull (New York: St Martin's, 1983), pp. 288–311.

Redick, Richard, "Patterns in the use of nursing homes by the aged mentally ill," National Institute of Mental Health Statistical Note No. 107 (Rockville, MD: NIMH, 1974).

Redick, R. W., and Witkin, M. J., "State and county mental hospitals, United States, 1979–80 and 1980–81," National Institute of Mental Health Statistical Note No. 165 (Rockville, MD: NIMH, 1983a).

——"Residential treatment centers for emotionally disturbed children in the United States, 1977–1980," National Institute of Mental Health Statistical Note No. 162 (Rockville, MD: NIMH, 1983b).

Robinson, Louis, *Should Prisoners Work?* (Philadelphia: Winston, 1931).

Rothman, David, *The Discovery of the Asylum: Social Order and Disorder in the New Republic* (Boston: Little, Brown, 1971).

——*Conscience and Convenience: The Asylum and its Alternatives in Progressive America* (Boston: Little, Brown, 1980).

Ruggie, Mary, *The State and Working Women* (Princeton: Princeton University Press, 1984).

Russell, William, *The New York Hospital: A History of the Psychiatric*

Service, 1771–1936 (New York: Columbia University Press, 1945).

Schneider, David, and Deutsch, Albert, *The History of Public Welfare in New York State, 1867–1940* (Chicago: University of Chicago Press, 1941).

Schwartz, I., Jackson-Beeck, M., and Anderson, R., "The 'hidden' system of juvenile control," *Crime and Delinquency*, 30 (1984), pp. 371–85.

Scull, Andrew, *Decarceration: Community Treatment and the Deviant – A Radical View* (Englewood Cliffs, NJ: Prentice Hall, [1977] 1984).

Sedgwick, Peter, *Psychopolitics* (London: Pluto, 1982).

Segal, S. P., and Aviram, U., *The Mentally Ill in Community-based Sheltered Care: A Study of Community Care and Social Integration* (New York: Wiley, 1978).

Shefter, Martin, "Party, bureaucracy, and political change in the United States," in *Political Parties: Development and Decay*, eds Louis Maisel and Joseph Cooper (Beverly Hills, CA: Sage, 1978), pp. 211–66.

Skocpol, Theda, "Political response to capitalist crisis: neo-Marxist theories of the state and the case of the New Deal," *Politics and Society*, 10 (1980), pp. 155–201.

——*States and Social Revolutions: A Comparative Analysis of France, Russia, and China* (Cambridge, UK: Cambridge University Press, 1979).

Skocpol, Theda, and Armenta, Edward, "Did capitalists shape social security?" *American Sociological Review*, 50 (1985), pp. 572–5.

Skowronek, Stephen, *Building a New American State: The Expansion of National Administrative Capacities, 1877–1920* (Cambridge, UK: Cambridge University Press, 1982).

Smith, C. J., and Hanham, R. Q., "Deinstitutionalization of the mentally ill: a time path analysis of American states, 1955–1975," *Social Science and Medicine*, 15 (1981), pp. 361–81.

Smith, R. A., *A Quiet Revolution – Probation Subsidy* (Washington DC: US Department of Health, Education, and Welfare, 1972).

Spector, Malcolm, "Beyond crime: seven methods to control trouble-some rascals," in *Law and Deviance*, ed. H. L. Ross (Beverly Hills, CA: Sage, 1981), pp. 127–58.

Staples, Clifford, "The politics of employment-based insurance in the United States," *International Journal of Health Services*, 19 (1989), pp. 415–31.

Staples, William, "Toward a structural perspective on gender bias in the juvenile court," *Sociological Perspectives*, 27 (1984), pp. 349–67.

——"Restitution as a sanction in juvenile court," *Crime and Delinquency*, 32 (1986), pp. 177–85.

——"Technology, control, and the social organization of work at a British hardware firm, 1791–1891," *American Journal of Sociology*, 93 (1987a), pp. 62–8.

——"Law and social control in juvenile justice dispositions," *Journal of Research in Crime and Delinquency*, 24 (1987b), pp. 7–22.

Staples, William, and Warren, Carol, "Mental health and adolescent social control," in *Research in Law, Deviance and Social Control: A Research Annual*, eds S. Spitzer and A. Scull (Greenwich, CT: JAI Press, 1988), pp. 113–26.

State of California, *Senate Interim Committee on the Treatment of Mental Illness*, First Partial Report (Sacramento, 1956a).

——*Senate Interim Committee on the Treatment of Mental Illness*, Second Partial Report (Sacramento, 1956b).

Stein, Herbert, *The Fiscal Revolution in America* (Chicago: University of Chicago Press, 1969).

Sutton, John, *Stubborn Children: Controlling Delinquency in the United States, 1640–1981* (Berkeley and Los Angeles: University of California Press, 1988).

Texas Penitentiary Committee, *Report of Findings* (Austin, 1913).

Thompson, J. W., Bass, R. D., and Witkin, M. J., "Fifty years of psychiatric services, 1940–1990," *Hospital and Community Psychiatry*, 33 (1982), pp. 711–17.

Tocqueville, Alexis de, *On Democracy, Revolution, and Society*, eds J. Stone and S. Mennell (Chicago: University of Chicago Press, 1980).

US Bureau of the Census, *Insane and Feeble-Minded in Hospitals and Institutions, 1904* (Washington DC: US Government Printing Office, 1906).

——*Insane and Feeble-Minded in Institutions, 1910* (Washington DC: US Government Printing Office, 1910).

——*Paupers in Almshouses, 1923* (Washington DC: US Government Printing Office, 1925).

——*Feeble-Minded and Epileptics in Institutions, 1923* (Washington DC: US Government Printing Office, 1926).

——*Statistical Abstract of the United States* (Washington DC: US Government Printing Office, 1930–1985).

——*Institutional Populations, 1950* vol. 4, Special Reports, part 2, chapter C (Washington DC: US Government Printing Office, 1953).

——*The Historical Statistics of the United States: Colonial Times to 1957* (Washington DC: US Government Printing Office, 1960).

——*Children in Custody* (Washington DC: US Government Printing Office, 1974–1985).

——*The Historical Statistics of the United States: Colonial Times to 1970* (Washington DC: US Government Printing Office, 1975).

——*Social Indicators, 1976* (Washington DC: US Government Printing Office, 1977).

US Bureau of Labor Statistics, *Convict Labor in 1923* (Washington DC: US Government Printing Office, 1925).

——*Employment and Payrolls, December 1940* Serial No. R1250 (Washington DC: US Government Printing Office, 1941).

US Congress Joint Economic Committee, "Privatization of prison construction in New York," Hearing of December 5, 1984 (Washington DC: US Government Printing Office, 1985).

US Department of Justice, *Sourcebook of Criminal Justice Statistics* (Washington DC: US Government Printing Office, 1985).

US Department of Labor, *Convict Labor, 1886* (Washington DC: US Government Printing Office, 1887).

US General Accounting Office, *Returning the Mentally Disabled to the Community: Government Needs to Do More* (Washington DC: General Accounting Office, 1977).

US Senate Committee on the Judiciary, *Ford Administration Stifles Juvenile Justice Policy* (Washington DC: US Government Printing Office, 1975).

US Social Security Administration, *Social Security Bulletin* (Washington DC: US Government Printing Office, 1980).

Vatter, Harold, *The US Economy in the 1950s: An Economic History* (Chicago: University of Chicago Press, 1963).

Vaux, Richard, *Notices of the Original and Successive Attempts to Improve the Discipline of the Prison at Philadelphia and to Reform the Criminal Code of Pennsylvania* (Philadelphia, 1826).

Vladeck, Bruce, *Unloving Care: The Nursing Home Tragedy* (New York: Basic, 1980).

Waldo, D. R., and Lazenby, H. C., "Demographic characteristics and health care use and expenditures by the aged in the United States, 1977–1984," *Health Care Financing Review*, 6 (1984), pp. 1–22.

Warren, Carol, "New forms of social control: the myth of deinstitutionalization," *American Behavioral Scientist*, 25 (1981), pp. 724–40.

——*Madwives: Schizophrenic Women in the 1950s* (Rutgers, NJ: Rutgers University Press, 1987).

Warren, Carol, and Staples, William, "Fieldwork in forbidden terrain: the state, privatization and human subjects regulations," *The American Sociologist* vol. 20 3 Fall (1989), pp. 267–77.

Weir, Margaret, and Skocpol, Theda, "State structures and the possibility for 'Keynesian' responses to the great depression in Sweden, Britain, and the United States," in *Bringing the State Back In*, eds P. Evans, DeiFrich Rueschemeyer, and Theda Skocpol (Cambridge: Cambridge University Press, 1985), pp. 107–63.

Witkin, Michael, "Trends in patient care episodes in mental health facilities, 1955–1977," National Institute of Mental Health Statistical Note No. 107. (Rockville, MD: NIMH, 1980).

Wolfe, Alan, *The Limits of Legitimacy* (New York: The Free Press, 1977).

Yoder, Dale, and Davies, George, *Depression and Recovery* (New York: McGraw-Hill, 1934).

Zenoff, Elyce, and Zients, Allan, "If civil commitment is the answer for children, what are the questions?" *The George Washington Law Review*, 51 (1983), pp. 171–214.

Zilboorg, G., and Henry, G., *A History of Medical Psychology* (New York: W. W. Norton, 1973).

Index